Grieving & Healing
Through the Prism of Torah;

a bereaved parent's spiritual journey beyond pain & grief

by Baruch C. Cohen
in loving memory of Hindy Cohen
in honor of her 14th Yahrtzeit

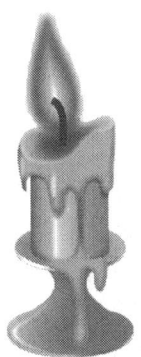

חנה הינדא בת ברוך חיים ועדינה כהן
נלב"ע ראש חודש אדר תשס"ד

חן ושכל טוב מצאה בעיני כל רואיה
נקטפה מאתנו מטרם י"ח שנותיה
השאירה לאנחות את כל אוהביה ואהוביה

הוקירה והעריצה את הוריה ומחנכיה
ישרה וצנועה במידותיה ובהליכותיה
נשמתה יצאה בטהרה ולא התלוננה על יסוריה
דבוקה וגאה בבית יעקב וחברותיה
אבדה לנו כלי חמדה ואין תמורה תחתיה

© **2017** by Baruch C Cohen Esq.
All rights reserved.
Email: baruchcohen@baruchcohenesq.com

Typesetting
Behindthedaf@gmail.com
+ 972 (0)533114757

Producer
Produced by Ramot Press
wedoseforim@gmail.com
www.ramotpress.com

In loving memory of Hindy Cohen Ob"m
Adar 1 5764 / February 23, 2004

You can shed tears that she is gone
or you can smile because she has lived.

You can close your eyes and pray that she'll come back
or you can open your eyes and see all she's left..

Your heart can be empty because you can't see her
or you can be full of the love you shared.

You can turn your back on tomorrow and live yesterday
or you can be happy for tomorrow because of yesterday.

You can remember her and only that she's gone
or you can cherish her memory and let it live on.

You can cry and close your mind, be empty and turn your back
or you can do what she'd want: smile, open your eyes, love and go...

Grieving & Healing

Table of Contents

Adar 1 5764 / February 23, 2004 3

Introduction: 14 years of Yahrtzeits 11

February 22, 2004: Strategies for Being Strong (the night before the tragedy) 13
    A Foundation of my Emunah and Bitachon is Never Losing Hope

February 24, 2004 / Adar 2 5764 My Hesped for Hindy, ...16

March 23, 2004, Hindy's Shelsohim 24
    "Sabeinu Mituvecha VeSamcheinu Bishuashecha"

    The Aish Kodesh's vort on Moshe Rabeinu's question to Hashem: "Will I truly cease to be remembered once I die?"

    She's in another place

    The Removal of Rabban Gamliel as the Prince and Head of the Yeshiva

June 1, 2004, My comments to the Chai Lifeline Circle of Friends at the home of Fred & Deena Leeds 35

February 10, 2005, Hindy's 1st Yahrtzeit, at the Cemetery 42

February 13, 2005, Comments at Hindy's Hachnosas Sefer Torah 44
    Painful Parallels

    "Gevilin Nisrophin Veosyious Porchos Be-Avir"

Klausenberg 50
    May 12, 2005, Letter to Rabbi Tzvi Elimelech Halberstam, Sanz Klauzenberger Rebbe of Kiryat Sanz Netanyah

    September 28, 2005, Response from the Sanz Klauzenberger Rebbe of Kiryat Sanz Netanyah, ISRAEL

November 30, 2005: Letter to Rabbi Tzvi Elimelech Halberstam the Sanz Klauzenberger Rebbe of Kiryat Sanz Netanyah, ISRAEL.............58

Grieving & Healing

May 20, 2005, comments to Orthodox Bereaved Parents Support Group in Teaneck, NJ 61

March 1, 2006, Chizuk to a group of Chai Lifeline parents 64
    "Never Despair of Hashem's Mercy" adaptions from the Sefer Techias Hameisim by the Biala Rebbe of Lugano Switzerland

April 9, 2006, Hindy's Hatzalah Ambulance Dedication 71

July 2006, Comments to a Group of Bereaved Parents, Westwood, CA, "If Only We Could See"...74

February 2007, Hindy's 3rd Yahrtzeit Seudah 82
    Miriam's Rebuke to Amram

    The Dubno Maggid's Moshol of Naive City Boys & Bread

    The Two Ships of Koheles Rabah

    Finding the Word "Nechamah" in the Torah

    "Rav Lach Sheves Be'emek Habocho"

    "Gezeirah Al Hameis Shenishtakech Min Halev"

June 2007, BYLA Graduation, Presentation of Hindy Cohen Middos Award..91

March 16, 2008, Comments at Mesivta of Greater Los Angeles School Trustee's Dinner...92
    Mercaz HaRav Tragedy

    The Klausenberger Rebbe's Insight

June 2008, BYLA Graduation, Presentation of Hindy Cohen Middos Award..95
    "Mishenichnas Adar Marbim B'simcha"

    The powerful metaphor of the Shattered Luchos

May 1, 2009, Halacha's Sensitivity to Bereaved Parents - the Halachic Prohibition of Kissing a Child in Shul During Davening.....99

Grieving & Healing

May 2009, Comments to a group of Orthodox Jewish Bereaved Parents 101

    Perspectives on Life in the World to Come; Through the Brilliant Prism of the Gesher Hachaim

        Insights of the Gesher Hachaim

        Rabbi Abie Rotenberg's Conversation in The Womb

        Midrash Tanchuma

        Rabbi Abie Rotenberg's Nishomele

        Colonel David (Mickey) Marcus

January 2010, Comments to a group of Bereaved Parents (non-Jewish) 115

    Mastering the Bounce

        The Fall

        The Impact

        Restoration

        Elevation

February 2010, Comments at Hindy's 6th Yahrtzeit Seudah 118

    The Nesivas Sholom on Sarah Imeinu's last minutes & the evil Satan's deadly trick

    "V'haseir Satan Milfaneinu U'meiachareinu"

February 2011, Hindy's 7th Yahrtzeit Seudah 123

    "Samcheinu Keeymos Inisani Shnos Rainu Raah"

    "Aderabah"

    "Vayidom Aharon"

June 24, 2011, A Message in a Bottle - the Gerrer Rebbe's Letter 129

Grieving & Healing

November 11, 2011 - Comments to a group of Bereaved Parents, quoting from The Jigsaw Puzzle; Kitchen Table Wisdom by Dr. Rachel Naomi Remen 132

February 2012, Hindy's 8th Yahrtzeit Seudah.................. 135
- It's Happening Again
- "Baruch Gozer U'mekayeim"
- Yaakov's Avinu's Silence
  - Yaakov's Harsh Response to Rochel's Plea for Children
  - Rochel Imeinu's Great Merit
  - Payback

February 2013, Hindy's 9th Yahrtzeit Seudah.................. 145
- Ki Azi "Vezimros" Kah
- Ben Oni vs Benyamin

July 28, 2013, Comments at Oscherowitz Sheva Berachos............... 152
- Broken: Why Breaking the Tablets Was Moshe Rabbeinu' Greatest Accomplishment
  - Broken
  - In the Fragments

September 13, 2013: Comments at Orthodox Jewish Bereaved Parents Support Group.................. 157
- Lesson of Survival Derived from an innocent Rashi in Parshas Pinchos

March 2014, Comments at Hindy's 10th Yahrtzeit.................. 160
- Binyomin's Consolation of Yaakov
- Binyomin's Silence
- Binyomin's Pain & Anguish Over Yosef
- Shevet Binyomin's Yashpeh Stone

March 2015, Comments at Hindy's 11th Yahrtzeit.................. 170

Grieving & Healing

"Vayidom Aharon" the Sounds of Silence

> Eighth Day
>
> It Should Have Been a Day of Joy
>
> What Could Aharon Have Said?
>
> Aharon's Reward (A Death Penalty Mitzvah?)
>
> Ironically, Hashem Tells Moshe to Be Quiet
>
> Perhaps by Being Quiet, Aharon Was Actually Speaking Volumes. The "Sounds of Silence."
>
> What Is the Message of Vayidom?
>
> "Be'damayikh Chayii"

March 5, 2016, Broken Heart & Shattered Luchos, Comments of Baruch Cohen in Observance of the 12th Yahrtzeit of Hindy Cohen 184

> Avinu Malkeinu: the Shoes of the Danube
>
> Broken
>
> Broken Hearts; Shattered Luchos
>
> Rising from the Ashes
>
> Turn to Nothing to Become Something
>
> Cracked Pots & the Art of Kintsukuroi

Shedding Tears over the Deaths of the Sons on Aharon Hakohein - Comments of Baruch Cohen in Observance of the 13th Yahrtzeit of Hindy Cohen.. 196

> Rav Akiva Eiger's Pure Dove
>
> Why Parshas Acharei Mos on Yom Kippur, and not Parshas Shemini?
>
> "V"
>
> Are you Looking in, or Looking Out?
>
> A Carrot, an Egg, and a Cup of Coffee

March 10, 1998: Hindy's Speech on the Meaning of Bas Mitzvah

Comments at the Kiddush of Chaya Chana Hindy, May 1, 2017...... 211

Bais Yaakov of Los Angeles - Hindy Cohen Memorial Fund 213

Grieving & Healing

Introduction: 14 years of Yahrtzeits

This *Machberes* and collection of my speeches was 14-years in the making. It's been 14 years since our beloved daughter Hindy died and moved on to the next world. Every year on the Shabbos before her Yahrtzeit, I would speak at Shalosh Seudos at Congregation Etz Chaim of Hancock Park before family and friends sharing original Torah thoughts of grief and healing in memory of Hindy.

The Shaarei Teshuvah in *Hilchos Meah Berachos* writes that after every Motzoi Shabbos when our Neshamah Yeseirah returns to Shomayim, Hashem rewards us for being MeChadesh Torah on Shabbos, by placing a crown on our father's head. I would like to think that in addition to the crown being placed on my father, Hashem puts a crown on Hindy's head too, for my attempts at being MeChadesh Torah on Shabbos in her memory.

What follows herein, is a collection of 14 years of these Chiddushei Torah that chart my spiritual journey beyond grief. It also includes my speeches at various Simchas as well. It is my hope that these words of Chizuk and Nechama uplift others going through difficult times; to transcend the trauma and reclaim Simcha in our lives. I do this in memory of Hindy.

You might know someone going through a hard time. You yourself might be experiencing a painful personal

Nisayon. This book is carefully designed to validate pain, and offer glimpses of hope. Sharing this book with a Chaver in emotional pain would be a tremendous Mitzvah and a Zechus for Hindy's memory.

While I was in the throes of my own tragedy, never in a million years did I ever dream that I would one day have the clarity to reclaim Simcha. My grief was a black hole that consumed my soul. While I was at ground zero, I was pain. and was synonymous with pain. But with God's help and through a lot of hard work, I went from being pain, to having pain. The pain migrated slowly out of my body and conscience. The book charts my personal growth through Torah insights.

Baruch Cohen

Los Angeles, CA

February 22, 2004: Strategies for Being Strong (the night before the tragedy)

It is now clear to me that I need to write to sort out my thoughts.

While this very bitter Nisayon dulls my mind and makes it very difficult to think and concentrate, at the same time, it also brings a certain acuity of perspective and clarity of thought during intermittent moments of calm between tears. It has awoken a very intense fear of Hashem in me that I never experienced before.

What follows are some random thoughts that are weighing heavy on me right now, and I feel a very strong urge to commit them to writing now - while I have them in my focus. Something instinctive inside of me akin to prophecy telling me to hold true to these powerful thoughts for they might serve me well down the road when things get worse.

A Foundation of my Emunah and Bitachon is Never Losing Hope

My family and I should not despair -- even in the face of this terminal stage of the illness, even when the doctors at CHLA give no chance for Hindy's survival. This of course, defies all logic. After all, I heard what I heard from the oncologists concerning the severity of the situation and I'm not in denial.

Yet, I have support for this and draw some strength from the Gemorah that I learned in the Daf Hayomi several years ago -- what R' Yochanan and R' Elazar said in Mesechta Berachos, in Perek Rishon of Mei'eimasi, Daf 10a: Afilu Cherev Chadoh

Munachas Al Tzavaro Shel Odom Al Yimnah Atzmo Min Horachamim "Even if a sharp sword lies on a person's neck he should not refrain from praying for mercy." Baruch Hashem I learned this Gemorah for it gives me strength during these dark times.

It is very important for me to focus on the fact that there is nothing beyond Hashem's ability. That the grim prognosis is not the ultimate reality -- but that what is happening is only through Hashem's will and He can change the laws of nature at any time. Is there anything beyond Hashem's ability? All is possible. Hashem is all-powerful. To Him, it makes no difference whether or not there are natural means of saving Hindy.

I truly believe that Hashem is testing me - He is bringing me to a point where there is no hope through natural means to test my belief in Him. And that Hindy's salvation will come at the last possible moment.

When I will be asked to give an accounting to Hashem at the and of my life, I will be judged by my lack of belief in Hashem's unlimited ability - especially now, where all human reason sees no hope. Therefore, I must trust in Hashem's capability now.

Without my Emunah and Bitachon, all will be lost. But just as the sword of the cancer is upon our necks (how ironic the metaphor given the location of the deadly tumor) I will continue to daven to Hashem. Even when all hope seems to be lost, I will continue to daven and hope and trust in Hashem, for there is yet hope.

But I must go further than that. What is happening to

Grieving & Healing

Hindy is beyond my understanding. I have to recognize the impossibility of understanding Hashem - yet to continue to put my faith in Him. I've got to ignore my personal doubts and achieve a stronger Emunah in Him.

I also have an ulterior motive in strengthening my belief in Hashem now. I'm hoping that it will have a therapeutic effect on me and help me proceed as a source of strength for my family, and ease the pain in my heart. Right now, my world appears very dark and my spirits broken. I have no doubt that these feelings come from lack of real solid belief and faith in Hashem. Because I don't really feel Hashem's Presence within me and just give lip service to Him, I feel continuously distressed and broken. I'm hoping that if I work on myself now, and truly believe in Hashem and His Hashgocha Peratis, that the painful road we are embarking on will not depress or break me. I will adopt Dovid Hamelech's pledge in Tehillim 23:4: *Gam ki Elech Begey Tzalmoves Lo Irah Ra Ki Ata Imadi.* "Even when I walk in the valley of the shadow of death, I fear no evil for You are with me.

February 24, 2004 / Adar 2 5764 My Hesped for Hindy,[1]

For years Adina and I dreamed of escorting our sweet beautiful Hindy to the Chupah. Never did we think we would be escorting our lovely Hindy to her Levayah.

On March 29, 1986, HKBH gave Adina and I a beautiful child, and she was given to us - in trust - as a Pikodon - for safekeeping, and we named this gift Chana Hinde. On February 23, 2004, HKBH demanded that we return to Him, that Pikodon whom we had held in trust for 17½ wonderful years.

There is some nechomo in our hearts in knowing that we returned Hindy to HKBH as a Bas Yisroel, that we faithfully honored the terms of our shemirah giving Hindy the proper chinuch and torah values.

Hindy was our life, our joy. Hindy was a *kodoshdicker* Neshama. She was a very holy soul.

She loved her family very much.

---

1. (My thoughts and feelings during the Hesped: *"Hindy: I feel like my heart has stopped; this moment is the moment that will stand as forever in my life. This is the last day that I will see you, and this is the last touch that I can give you. I lay my face on your coffin and wonder where is your head so that I can give you a kiss. You're a body without a Neshomah. I know your Neshomah has gone somewhere else; is no longer with us. How will we live without you? This is a moment of sheer terror for me; the pain is so intense that I feel that my soul has left my body. I am disconnected from my limbs, from my heart, my breathing. Parents should not have to watch their daughter die. I should've died before you. Parents should not have to bear witness to the terrible fact that as much as we love you, we couldn't protect you from the illness that claimed your life."*

Grieving & Healing

Hindy was a Bas Yisroel, the perfect Bais Yaakov girl. For Hindy being in Bais Yaakov High School was not a mere issue of student pride at their alma mater. Bais Yaakov defined Hindy. She was its very proud ambassador. Hindy loved her teachers at BYLA but there are three that Hindy had a very special kesher with and I would like to mention them by name (and I do not mean to exclude anyone): To Mrs Bursztyn, Mrs. Bess, & Mrs. Wolmark I hope you all know how much Hindy loved you and enjoyed you. I envy your schar in olom habah for giving Hindy the love of learning Torah. When nurses in the hospital marveled at Hindy's Derech Eretz, at her refined Middos, and of her ehrlichkeit, Hindy took pride in explaining what it meant to be a Bais Yaakov girl. During Hindy's 2½ years of illness, what pained her the most, was her missing out on being with her friends at Bais Yaakov.

It is hard to describe the Simcha in our home and at Bais Yaakov when Hindy returned at the very end of 10th grade after her 1st bout with cancer. With teachers and classmates running up to her, hugging her and kissing her. And all the while Hindy wanting to lay low and not draw any attention to herself.

And when it hit a 2nd time, and we endured the difficulties of a life-threatening stem cell transplant, and Hindy missed out on the end of 1th grade and the 1st half of her senior year, what she wished for most, was to be back in school with her friends.

Imagine the difficulty for us, when at the beginning of this year, I prepaid Hindy's tuition, and shook hands with Rabbi Bursztyn that Hindy should be zoche to experience Bais Yaakov as a senior. So at the end of February of this year, when Hindy returned to Bais Yaakov, the simcha was not to be believed. It was if Adar came earlier.

This past Shabbos was the Bais Yaakov Shabbaton in Malibu. We had known already the preceding Monday that the tumor returned again. How Hindy yearned to participate in it and to be with her friends.

Notwithstanding her difficulties breathing, and her knowledge of the returned tumor, Hindy decided to be with her friends for a beautiful shabbos that she said to us afterwards meant a lot to her. It is impossible to describe the turmoil in our hearts letting Hindy go this past Shabbos to be with her friends.

So we will be doing something regal and noble for Hindy after the funeral. We will proceed from here to Bais Yaakov, to Hindy's school, and to bring Hindy one last time to her school that she loved so much, to bring the Bas Yisroel back to her Bais Yaakov one last time. We will proceed to the cemetery from there.

Last week on Monday, we all knew that the tumor returned with a vengeance. We were so surprised and shocked by the severity and the suddenness of the news -- since the January 5, 2004 CT-scan showed that everything was clear. On that date I recall making a private Lechaim with Hindy - celebrating this great moment to give her hope for the future. So for the last week, we walked with a heavy burden on our heads, all the while knowing what was in store for Hindy. And yet, this past Shabbos was the BYLA Shabbaton, and Hindy was determined to go and participate. We didn't want Hindy out of our sights, and we of course wanted to keep her home this shabbos, to maximize our time together. But we decided that what's best

Grieving & Healing

for Hindy is that she be with her friends for Shabbos, so we put aside our own needs, and with very heavy hearts, we let her go to the Shabbaton. It was a very difficult thing for us to do. Looking back with hindsight being 20/20, Adina and I are glad that Hindy's last beautiful experience was with her friends at the BYLA shabbaton.

To my Hindy: Mommy and I knew for a week that the situation was critical and terminal. We suspected that you did to, after all you are a bright intelligent and intuitive person. But we decided to keep the - severity - of the situation from you to protect you from feeling -- that all was lost because we love you. And Mommy and I davened to Hashem with all our hearts to have Rachmonus on you and spare you from the pain that we feared was in store for you. As of Sunday, your situation became worse and worse, and the paramount thought by Mommy and I was to relieve you of your suffering. Yesterday morning, on Rosh Chodesh Adar, with the blessings of Daas Torah, we added a name to you -- the name Ruchomo - in the hopes that HKBH will have compassion on you and on us and take away your Tzaar. And he did. And we must thank HKBH for answering our Tefilos and returning Hindele's Neshama to shomayim quickly.

We were in your bedroom yesterday, and when you stopped breathing, you will recall Mommy crying out "Hindy I love you, I love you, I love you."

Hindy, when you go to Shomayim, I want you to know how much we love you and we want you to take our love for you, with you.

Grieving & Healing

To my Adina, words cannot describe your pain, a mother could never have cared for a child better than you did for Hindy. You surrounded her with constant love. No matter how debilitating and exhausting the process, one thing was constant: in front of Hindy you were always smiling. When Hindy looked at her Mommy for strength, she saw a loving mother, saying Tehillim everyday, with a calm, soothing and beautiful smile that always said: "It's going to be ok." Even yesterday, when things weren't going well at all, she did look at you and you managed to smile to her reassuringly. May HKBH give you the strength to get through this.

To my children: Yehuda, Tali and Shaya: We all know how much Hindy loved you. Her room is festooned with pictures of you. She took great pride in being your big sister and role model. Yehuda, right before your Bar Mitzvah, when Hindy relapsed, it meant so much to Hindy that she was able to make it to your Simcha. And I know how much it meant to you. To Tali and Shaya, it's very hard to lose a sister, but Aba and Mommy want you to always remember Hindy and how much she loved you.

To my mother-in-law: Adina's mother, Hindy's Bubbie: I don't need to tell you how much Hindy loved you. You know. She loved everything about you. You were the one zoiche to be with her when her Neshama departed. I know how difficult this is for you. I also do not need to tell you Aba, how much Hindy loved you as well. When you were around, Hindy felt safe. You reassured her and made her always feel great.

There are so many people in our lives whom we want to thank for enriching Hindy's life. Hindy would have wanted to thank

Grieving & Healing

them personally as well. There is always a risk of naming names at the risk of forgetting one. I apologize in advance if I accidentally failed to mention you.

Rabbi Hershy Ten of the Bikur Cholim: Hershy: When darkness descended on our family, and Hindy was 1st diagnosed with cancer, an angel in human form came into our lives, and his name is Hershy Ten. Reb Hershy, my yedid, my close chaver, directed us and advised us through an endless maze of doctor visits, 2nd and 3rd opinions, xrays, MRI's, CT's scans, blood and platelette drives, with love and compassion 24/7 for 2½ years. He would constantly remind us that he's working so hard for us as if Hindy was his own. In fact, Hershy, you know what a special relationship you had with Hindy. When we were hospitalized and you walked the miles every Shabbos, every yom tov to visit us, how her beautifil blue eyes would lighten up when you entered the room. Hershy: *Imo Anochi Betzorah*. Hershy: you know that we made a pledge to one another - that at Hindy's Chasunah that you will have a mitzvah tance with Hindy. That pledge sustained me through many a dark moment. There are no words to express our love and thanks to you Hershy. No words.

To the many selfless people -- hundreds of you -- who gave anonymously blood and platelettes to Hindy. This was a *Chesed Shel Emes* that saved Hindy's life hundreds of times to which we are eternally grateful..

To the blood organizers at Bikur Cholim Matty Low and Nechama Kram - who we affectionately referred to as Draculas -- we know that you were doing your jobs, but you went *lifnim meshuras hadin* and helped us immeasurably..

Grieving & Healing

To the many dedicated volunteers of Chai Lifeline, words fail me.

To her doctors at Kaiser and CHLA: HKBH chose you to be His messengers of cure. We believe that G-d held your hand and guided you during your treatments of Hindy.

To Loraine Spira: No one our age connected with Hindy like Loraine Spira. She swooped into our lives, visiting us in the hospital – every day. Bringing us food, talking to Adina and most importantly to Hindy as well. Giving Hindy the chills for hours, all the while talking to Hindy, soothing her soul. And when doctors walked into the room, Loraine quietly disappeared from the room waiting quietly outside - never to intrude on Hindy's privacy. This is something, Loraine, that Hindy told me herself, she appreciated so much about you.

Her friends: Rochella Rubin, Naomi Twersky, Sarah Jacobs, Tomy Katz, Leba Friedman, Mimi Gohare, Ahuva Dena Friedman, Tovah Abrahamson, Chava Leah Zyskind, and I'm sorry if I left anyone out. You know how much Hindy loved you. We felt it all the time.

There is one friend, in particular, whom we must give *Hakaras Hatov* and Hindy would have wanted it and would have wanted to say good bye: Adina and I want to express our love to our dear Sarah Jacobs. Sarah, Adina and I love you, and we know how difficult this is for you. You were an amazing friend to Hindy. You were with her every minute. When Hindy felt uncomfortable you always were there to ease things for her. When Hindy couldn't talk after a painful surgery, you were happy to just sit there with her quietly looking at each other.

Grieving & Healing

I won't embarrass you publically and remind you of all of the many Chassodim that you did for Hindy, but they were all known by us, acknowledged and very much appreciated. Last night, Adina tried to call you, but as soon as you picked up and Adina heard your voice on the phone, she started crying and couldn't continue. She couldn't talk. Hindy will return to shomayim with the collective love of her good friends.

To our beautiful family of brothers, sisters, uncles and aunts, and cousins, we can't begin to thank you for the support and help.

It's hard to say my farewell to my Hindy. Mommie and I love you very much. We love you. We love you. We love you.

March 23, 2004, Hindy's Shelsohim

I've been struggling these past few weeks to know what to say today. What could one say? What is more precious to every parent than their child? How much love does every parent have for every single child? Hindy, my love for you during your too brief 17 years was enormous, and it has only continued to grow during this past month since your Petirah. Not a single day, not a single hour, and probably not even a single minute has gone by during this entire month without my thinking of you repeatedly. Wherever I go, I see you. I've even tried calling you on your private line, hoping that you would pick up so that I can hear your sweet beautiful voice. How can one deal with such a void and what can one say about it? I've been grappling this entire month for some way to deal with this huge loss, this gaping wound in my heart. The absence of Hindy in my life. The absence of Hindy in our lives.

"Sabeinu Mituvecha VeSamcheinu Bishuashecha"

In every Shabbos Tefilah we ask Hashem - "*Sabeinu Mituvecha*" - "satiate us from Your goodness" and "*Samcheinu Bishuashecha*" - "make us happy with your salvation". The obvious question is - shouldn't both of these happen automatically? In other words, if the good that occurs to us is truly from Hashem, won't it necessarily satiate us. And if Hashem is really the source of our salvation, it should certainly make us happy! The question that bothered me, therefore, was - What are we really asking for in these Tefilahs? The answer that I came to was - even that which is really Hashem's own good and salvation isn't always

Grieving & Healing

so obviously easy to appreciate. These Tefilahs are, therefore, asking Hashem for help to be able to see the true good within whatever occurs to us, whether it is easy to perceive or whether it may be very difficult to see.

I was also struck by the fact that these 2 requests follow immediately after our Tefilah to Hashem - *"v'Sein Chelkeinu b'Sorasecha"* -"and grant us a portion in your Torah". I believe that it is this juxtaposition which is really the key to the Tefilah as well as being a powerful idea in its own right. What is the essential prerequisite for us to be able to see the goodness even in those events that are very challenging and painful? Only having a portion in Hashem's Torah.

This is certainly an important Tefilah that makes a great deal of sense, and I felt it's particular relevance to me *vis-a-vis* Hindy's illness, and now, Petirah. All throughout the over 2½ years of various treatments and procedures, short stays in the hospital and very long periods of time in the hospital, virtually every Shabbos - this Tefilah was in many ways my point of reference and my anchor. It was my opportunity every Shabbos to ask Hashem to help me, through the Torah I was learning to see and feel the good within our numerous painful and difficult challenges.

It has continued to be just as relevant to me during this past month, although in a very different and profound way. Until now I was asking Hashem to help me to cope with the numerous ongoing challenges in my life through His Torah. This past month I have been asking for the Torah to help me to deal with loss, the greatest loss that any parent could imagine.

Grieving & Healing

The Aish Kodesh's vort on Moshe Rabeinu's question to Hashem: "Will I truly cease to be remembered once I die?"

One of the ways that the Torah was able to help me very significantly this past month was through a beautiful essay that I was very fortunate to see. It was from a sefer called the "Aish Kodesh"- the "Holy Fire" which I was given shortly after Hindy passed away. The "Aish Kodesh" is an incredible work in many different ways. The holy Rebbe of Piazeczna, Harav Kalonymous Kalman Shapiro, zt'l, wrote the inspirational manuscript during his tenure as Rebbe of the Warsaw Ghetto. Shortly before the Ghetto was liquidated, the Rebbe buried his writings beneath the rubble with the hopeful plea that, after the war, they be taken to the Land of Israel. While they are all beautiful and inspirational, there is one that I found to be particularly relevant to my quest for consolation in regards to my daughter's untimely passing - and ironically, it is to be found in the sefer at Parshas Pekudei (this past week's parsha): It is by far the single most powerful and compelling source of Nechomo that I have encountered, and I feel it is befitting to share it with you tonight. It's relevance and application to Hindy's memory will become self-evident:

The Aish Kodesh discusses an emotional and touching Medrash that tells us that Moshe Rabeinu expressed a deep fear to Hashem - He asked: "Will I truly cease to be remembered (ie., amongst the Jewish people) once I die?" Hashem responded to Moshe Rabbeinu: "Just as you are standing here today and commanding the Jewish people to do the Mitzvah of the

Grieving & Healing

Shekalim (along with all the rest of the Mitzvos), it will similarly be as if you will be standing together with the Jewish people as they carry out the Mitzvah of the Shekalim every single year (in the future) and physically participating alongside them. {The Torah hints at this by expressing the Mitzvah of Shekalim as "Ki Sisah" - "when you will take the Shekalim (ie., in the future)", and not "Sah" - "take the Shekalim (ie., now in the present)".} The obvious question, however, is - "How could Moshe Rabeinu possibly be concerned about being forgotten by the Jewish people? He is constantly being mentioned all throughout the Torah!

In order to explain this, we need to understand a concept discussed by the Zohar Hakodosh - that Hashem "desires", so to speak, to dwell within the heart of every single Jew. This "desire" has 2 different aspects to it: i. Relationship with every Jew as a result of Hashem's great love for them; ii. Revelation through every Jew - only possible in the realm of physical action.

Similar to this "desire" of Hashem, so to speak, is a parallel desire from every Neshama (soul) that has passed away from this world to similarly maintain a relationship with those still dwelling in this physical world of action. Every Neshama rises to a much higher level in Gan Eden following their having been in this physical world than before it - since the essential revelation of Kedushah (sanctity) on the individual level is exclusively through the physical fulfillment of Mitzvos in this world. Therefore, besides the saying of Kaddish and the learning of Mishnayos for those that have passed away, it is a tremendous kindness for these Neshamos when we additionally keep them in mind as we are actually involved in doing Mitzvos and learning Torah. We should not merely try to remember them, but rather bind ourselves to them in order to actually do the Mitzvah and learn the Torah in partnership with them. They will thereby become "clothed" (in a sense) with a body and in the realm of action - capable of learning Torah and doing Mitzvos (once again) and thereby revealing a much greater level of Kedushah.

If Hashem Himself desires, so to speak, to dwell within the heart of every single Jew, all the more so every departed soul! - what an incredible kindness it therefore becomes to allow some aspect of them to reside (once again) within the midst of the Jewish people, to (actually) be engaged in Torah and Mitzvot together with them.

This thereby explains Moshe Rabeinu's concern - "Will I cease to be remembered (ie., amongst the Jewish people) once I die? The numerous references to Moshe Rabeinu in the Torah are all, of course, only dealing with him while he was alive - ie., as someone that had previously lived in the past. Moshe's question was specifically - "After I die, will it also be possible for me to be remembered in the present?" - ie., to exist within every single Jew and to continue to be engaged with Torah and Mitzvot together with them?

This was the question which Hashem responded to by reassuring Moshe Rabeinu - "Just as you are standing here today and commanding the Jewish people to do the Mitzvah of the Shekalim (along with all the rest of the Mitzvos), it will similarly be as if you will be standing together with the Jewish people as they carry out the Mitzvah of the Shekalim

Grieving & Healing

every single year (in the future) and physically participating alongside them.

The beautiful message that this contains is that - not only is Hindy right now in an incredible place of elevation and closeness to Hashem, but we actually have the ability to continue our relationship with her, specifically with our Torah and Avodas Hashem at Bais Yaakov. During her life, her thoughts and desires were unusually elevated, now they are certainly enormously greater. What is she now lacking? A physical body to carry out her elevated aspirations in terms of physical actions in this present world of action. And this is exactly what we can give to her.

It is therefore with bittersweet tears and a heavy heart that constantly yearns for Hindy's well-being that we announce the inauguration of the Hindy Cohen Memorial Fund at Bais Yaakov to perpetuate Hindy's memory and "bind" her to various programs of Torah & Chesed here.

It is very befitting that Hindy's memorial be at Bais Yaakov. Bais Yaakov is what defined Hindy. This is where Hindy lived as a true Bas Yisroel. This is where she yearned to return to when she was physically precluded by her illness. And while her hospital window faced the Hollywood Hills, to Hindy, it was facing Bais Yaakov. Hindy wore her Bais Yaakov uniform with pride and chashivus that she was a Bais Yaakov girl.

We are also pleased to announce that every year at graduation, the school will be awarding the Chana Hindy Cohen Middos Award to a graduate who has exemplary and refined Middos Tovos - all in Hindy's memory. The names of the recipients of this beautiful yearly award will be prominently placed in the Friedman/Mandelbaum library.

What an incredible kindness it therefore becomes to allow Hindy's Neshomoh to reside (once again) within the Kedushadik halls of Bais Yaakov, to actually be engaged in Torah and Mitzvos here, together with her friends.

Hindy, Mommy and I, have worked very hard this past month to maintain our relationship with you. Everything we did was done with your eternal merit in mind, to carry out on your behalf what you are no longer capable of physically doing yourself.

She's in another place

There is one particular analogy that I have returned to throughout this past month that has helped and comforted me. I try to imagine what it must have been like for a family in Europe a couple hundred years ago whose child had made aliya to Eretz Yisroel. While they knew that they would most likely never see their child again, they were comforted by the fact that their child was now in a much more elevated place. They certainly missed them terribly, but felt a satisfaction that as parents they had done all that they could have for them. They further understood that their child's life had been very meaningful and had merited to achieve its purpose to a very high degree.

The Torah, of course, expects Olam Haba to be as real to us as Eretz Yisrael was to European Jews 200 years ago. It may not be easy, but as Jews we need to see this as one of our fundamental

Grieving & Healing

obligations.

The second Mishnah of Pirke Avos tells us that the world stands on 3 pillars : Torah, Avodah, and Gemilus Chasadim. I was thinking that you, Hindy, have a level of Avodah - closeness and relationship to Hashem, right now that we in this physical world can only dream about. And the other 2 pillars that you are no longer capable of being involved in, Torah and Chessed, are exactly the 2 areas that Mommy and I will continue to work hard to cultivate and dedicate to your merit at Bais Yaakov. This way you are, hopefully, able to continue your growth and elevation in all areas.

The final inspiration which emerges from the essay in the Aish Kodesh is that not only are we able to continue our giving to Hindy, but that Hindy can actually continue to give to us. Various things that happened during Shiva and during the Sheloshim, were only possible through the elevation and inspiration we directly received from Hindy.

Hashem should grant our entire family and her friends the Heavenly assistance to actively maintain our relationship with our daughter, Hindy, *a"h* through greater and greater involvement and dedication to Torah and Mitzvos. And Hashem should help it to be a 2-way relationship as much as is possible - with her elevating us to greater and greater heights in terms of our actions in this world, while we provide the physical vehicle for her Neshamah to continue to grow more and more closely in the world of complete truth and clarity to HaKadosh Buruch Hu.

The Removal of Rabban Gamliel as the Prince and Head of the Yeshiva

There is a story in the Talmud (Gemora Berachos) that I had learned that keeps running through my head. It tells of how the Sages, for various reasons, decided to remove Rabban Gamliel as the Prince and Head of the Yeshiva. Looking for a replacement, they settled on Rabbi Elazar ben Azariya. When they offered him the position, he consulted his wife, who asked him a pointed question. "What do you need this for? How do you know that they won't throw you out tomorrow, just as they threw Rabban Gamliel out today?"

I had understood Rabbi Elazar ben Azariya's reply as follows. "And if they do remove me? So what if I occupy the position for only one day? Does it mean that it has no value? Absolutely not! From that day on, my whole outlook on life will be different and improved. Everything will take on new meaning. I'll know what it feels like to be the Prince, the Head of the Yeshiva. From that one day, I'll have memories that will last a lifetime. Everything I look at will be from a different perspective, a more meaningful one, because of the moments I served in that capacity. Are you saying that, just because an experience won't last forever, it means that it has no value? That, since I might have to give it up, I should never know the experience in the first place? That it won't be worth every second because it will have to end?! Heaven forbid!"

I feel exactly the same way about Hindy.

Hashem gives us many gifts in life. Some are long-term; others are short-term. Each child is a precious gift from Him.

Grieving & Healing

I sincerely hope and pray that the three gifts He has given me, will be long-term ones, for 120 years. But the 1st gift He gave me was a short-term one. And she was a gift that I really thought I would never have for as long as I did. We had 2.5 years of extended life with Hindy. So, what should I do? Should I sit here and be angry, and complain to Hashem because He cheated me? Or should I sit and be grateful for every single day of the free, short-term gift He bestowed upon us? The first 17 years we had Hindy was wonderful even with her illness. They were all wonderful, special days that, at one point or another, I didn't think would ever be. The challenge for us is not whether we will be angry with Hashem or harbor complaints against Him. The challenge is whether we have the capacity and ability to appreciate every special moment He gave us.

One of the hardest parts of our loss is explaining all this to Hindy's brothers and sisters. The sister that they had loved so much had been taken away from them. They each had their own private, personal relationship with her, and each one grieves deeply, but differently. There are many different meals being served in our house these days; no one is eating the same lunch. I try to help them deal with it as positively as possible. I tell them to imagine if Hashem would have gathered the whole world together and said, "I have a special girl I need someone to take care of and love. But, I have to tell you in advance--I'm only going to give her for 17 years. Who's willing to take her?" Knowing now how special she was, and how much she meant to us, would we have ever let anyone else even try to get her? Imagine if, 17 years ago, He would have looked into the future and seen how sad we are and how much we miss her. What if

He would have decided that it's not fair for us to feel so much sorrow; so, to spare us, He was going to give her to some other family? All of my children agree. We wouldn't want to have missed her for anything in the world.

Shaya once asked me "Why did Hindy die?" I told him that Hashem had a special girl whom he had to send down to live. However, she was so special, and He would miss her so much, that He couldn't bear to be apart from her for long. So, He was only going to send her away for 17 years. She didn't want to be away from him either, even for so short a time, but He told her she had to go. As a consolation, He promised her that He would find the very bestest, the very lovingest, the very specialest family, who would love her and hold her and take the very best care of her. Together, they looked down at all the families in the world. with all the brothers and sisters, and they chose our family for Hindy.

Grieving & Healing

June 1, 2004, My comments to the Chai Lifeline Circle of Friends at the home of Fred & Deena Leeds

On February 8, 2004, I had the opportunity and pleasure to speak before the Chai Lifeline Circle of Friends in its Board room on Pico Boulevard, about what Chai Lifeline meant to our family, having then, a child with a terminal illness.

As many of you are aware, our 17 year old daughter Hindy was stricken with a deadly cancer called Ewing's Sarcoma. Hindy's fight with cancer consumed nearly 3 of the last 17 years of her short life. Despite her failing health, a parent's hope for the future of their child never fails, and the tragedy of her death on 2/23/04 has been nearly impossible to acknowledge, let alone prepare for.

Many of you were kind enough to pay us shiva calls during our Aveilus - our spiritual journey beyond grief to consolation.

I hope that you appreciate how difficult it is for me to stand before you today, to talk about our experiences with Hindy's illness ... and death vis-a-vis Chai Lifeline.

Then, on 2/8/04, when I last spoke to this wonderful group. Hindy was in our lives. Today, she is gone. And I'm left with the pain of seeing Hindy's friends and knowing that they are alive and my lovely beautiful Hindy is not. It's the pain of losing my future with Hindy, of losing Hindy's future, and my own, somehow tied together. While she was alive, I imagined Hindy with a future of happiness. Now I will never see her High School graduation, her choice of husband, her children, her choice of career. How her face would have turned into a woman's face. It's the pain of Hindy not being there for her brothers and sisters.

So this is a difficult moment for me, indeed.

Prior to Hindy's illness, prior to the tidal wave of life hitting us, we were like most of you; protected and shielded from the notion that our children are very ill and may die from their illnesses. we even avoided looking at Chai Lifeline advertisements, because we couldn't bring ourselves to look at this kind of tragedy of pediatric illnesses that went terminal. When we saw a terminally ill child, we looked away. And I guess that's normal, because it's so much more comfortable and easy not having to face other people's nightmares.

That was then. When we were stricken with cancer, our lives changed and our perspectives changed 180 degrees.

We have since come to the realization that There are two worlds: (i) the world of cancers and the world of Chai Lifeline; & (ii) the outside world untouched by cancer. Thank God you live in the 2nd world.

What goes on inside the world of pediatric cancer - inside the world of Chai Lifeline - is simply indescribable. One cannot fathom that world from the outside. Yes, you can temporarily obtain a guest visa to visit our world, and you can even try as hard as you can to share the emotional pain and frustration to some extent, but you will never really get in, and you will never really feel it.

And It's nothing personal, but you will never really know what it's like - Thank God. Your well-intentioned visit to the BMT

Grieving & Healing

unit will end, you will have done your civic duty, you will have shown that you are a true friend doing whatever you can for us, but then you will exit the portal between our universes, and go home to your world, thanking God that it's not you or your child in the pediatric oncology ward of the hospital. You might even shed a tear, but will soon dry it up as you reemerge to the surface of the real world, where you have to deal with normal stuff like tuition, carpools and what's for dinner. Your instinct and natural survival will prevent you from getting too close to our world ... because it is just too scary to really entertain, and too devastating to place yourself ... in our shoes. So you will emotionally distance and numb yourself from the world of cancer, from the world of the Chai Lifeline so that you do not lose it and freak out. I was there, so I know.

And to those of us who are trapped in the prison cell of cancer and its aftermath, there is no escape, there is never an escape, there is no vacation, there is no distraction, and there is nowhere to turn -- but to face the unthinkable on a daily basis, 24/7.

We have been in this world of cancer since September 2001 (it's hard to believe). Prior to that, I was like you, in your world, happily oblivious to the world of pediatric illnesses, of the Chai Lifelines. rarely peeking behind the forbidden curtain. When I would read about pediatric cancers or I would see a Chai Lifeline advertisement, I quickly turned the page, because blocking it out of my mind was easier and safer than exposing myself to the pain and anguish that someone out there was going through. Looking back, I am not proud of the fact that I tried to avoid thinking about it. Perhaps I should have shared the burdens of my friends, but I was just too cowardice to do so.

You should understand that the bizarro world of cancer has its own unique vocabulary, in that, words that are tossed about between us and with our oncologists, have clinical importance to us. We've gotten over the initial shock that these harsh words create. The first time one hears the words "cancer" "tumor" "malignant" "relapse" "oncologist "relapse; "chemotherapy" "radiation" "BMT" "stem cell" "blood counts' 'and even the words: 'Chai-Lifelines' they detonate powerful shock waves throughout the body and mind. But we got over it. After a while, living with it, coping with it, and getting through it, we used these words routinely, perhaps even too comfortably. (I recall when I only practiced bankruptcy law, I had complete conversations with colleagues in coded terms: "I did a 2004 on a DIP for a 727 only to realize that I had a better cause of action in 523 which I then settled with a 7029 motion and a waiver of Rule 11" and no one outside of our narrow bankruptcy world understood what on earth they meant). We, in the world of cancer understand what these words mean … … but you really don't. You can't. Because you're not in it.

These words must sound scarier to you, scarier than they really are to us. So no matter how close you are to us, and how wonderful a friend you are to us, when you hear about BMT transplants and the like, you do not really hear it and do not really understand it, in the same way that we do. It sounds more horrible to you.

Grieving & Healing

During Hindy's illness, my wife and I were bone weary. We felt bereft. We were left incredulous, speechless, bewildered, adrift, inconsolable, and above all, abandoned. Our greatest fears were becoming reality.

We were paralyzed and motionless, perched precariously above a bottomless gorge. We were unable to concentrate, we felt irritable, restless and unwilling to talk. We stared but did not hear; we heard but did not listen. We muttered shallow greetings but we were hardly there. Instead, we were adrift in a sea of nothingness. We had few desires, little to no appetite, no interest in even being helped. We were literally dead inside. Nothing mattered but Hindy. We wanted to be left alone.

Most of our friends meant well. They tried to help. Many told us that they felt a moral duty to help us, but they typically performed their duties to us mindlessly, stammering an awkward hello, rambling through a good-bye, and then just glad to get out of our room at Pediatric Oncology. Thanking G-d that it wasn't their 17-year old in that bone marrow transplant unit. Our friends had no real plan or agenda for interacting with us, for choosing words that could be reassuring. They cared deep but thought shallow. I guess we are all clumsy at this business of helping families with terminally ill children, not because we don't care, but because we believe that there is nothing intelligent or effective that we can really say or do anyway.

And that is why Chai Lifeline is so critical. It fills such a major chasm and void. They are in the business of helping families with terminally ill children, because they believe that there are many intelligent and effective things to do and say - to help.

Grieving & Healing

I can tell you that they were like Vultures swooping from the sky. Helping, volunteering, assisting, supporting, loving. They knew and understood our new language of fear. They knew of the different language that we spoke. They knew of the new kind of oxygen that we breathed. They knew of the feelings of isolation that a family goes through. They knew of the collateral damage that a pediatric illness can have on siblings. They knew of treating illness with love - head on. Direct. Treating an illness with love. With no awkwardness, no stammering, just unconditional love.

They knew about the need to feed members of a family trapped in a hospital for shabbos, for yom tov, for every day of the week. No matter how complicated the menu, no matter how late in the day, no matter how many minutes right before shabbos, chai lifeline's answers were always: "It will be our pleasure to help you." From the food, to building a sukkah for us at home, to chanukah gifts to our kids, to parties, to retreats, to baseball games - all sponsored by Chai Lifeline.... They knew how to make everyone in the family feel loved.

Just as an aside, perhaps we take for granted a simple baseball game. It costs us virtually nothing to go. But do you know what it means to a family beset by tragedy who are paralyzed by the weight of their situation, to be able to get out and go to a simple Fahrkakte baseball game? Do you know what it means? I can assure that the seats are the worst in the Dodger stadium, but to us, they were like in Gan Eden. Because the look of the children's faces and of their parents, at the relief of getting out, spoke volumes - of the greatness of chai lifeline's efforts to think of the patients' and their family's needs.

Grieving & Healing

And can you imagine what it means to a family ... to know that selfless people like Helena Usdan & Corrine Kin organized a community-wide chol hamoed event solely for chai lifeline - and a chance to get out and enjoy a day like everyone else?

And can you imagine what it means to a family ... when a Marylin Sochachewksi from Santa Monica ... who doesn't even know us, comes to our hospital room at CHLA at the unpleasant corner of Sunset and Vermont to see how our child os doing?

And can you imagine what it means to a family... when they learn that in Bel Air, a group of caring people gave of their time and money to cross the threshold of caring to allow themselves to feel the pain of another, and to share in the burden of their friends, and to support Chai Lifeline?

Tonight I get to say Thank You to Rabbi Scholar and to Randy Grossman

Nowithstanding our loss, we will always be Chai Lifeline parents, and tonight, I thank you for all of your efforts on its behalf.

Grieving & Healing

February 10, 2005, Hindy's 1st Yahrtzeit, at the Cemetery

Hindy: Today is your 1st Yahrtzeit, and we are here to say Tehillim by your Kever. Hindy, my love for you during your too brief 17 years was enormous, and it has only continued to grow during this past year since your Petirah. Not a single day and not a single hour has gone by during this entire year without my thinking of you repeatedly. Wherever I go, I see you. I miss you terribly.

The Alter of Slobodka asked a question: We say in Shemoneh Esrei: "*Vezocher Chasdei Avos*" that Hashem remembers the Chesed of our Avos. Now we know the Chesed of Avrohom Avinu. But what Chesed did Yizchok Avinu do? We don't see anywhere in the Torah a Chesed that Yitzchok did. And the Alter of Slobodka gives an answer. He said that Yitzchok taught Klal Yisroel what it means to give up one's life. He taught us the Akeidah. When he showed us that he was willing to die because the Ribbono Shel Olom wanted that to happen. That was the greatest Chesed that he could've taught. That generations that followed his example until this very day. Because he taught us that a person can be Mekadesh Shem shomayim in the ultimate way.

So it occurred to me that based on what the Alter of Slobodka said, that even though there's Zechus Avos, but because of Yitzchok Avinu, Tzadikim and Tzidkonious were taken from us, such as Hindy, and she taught us and showed us. And it's because of Hindy that we are alive today. She's the one. We live in her Zechus. She lived and she died because she was taught by Yitzchok Avinu. So maybe we don't have anymore the zechus of Yitzchok Avinu, but we have the zechus of Hindy, because she had her own Akeidah, and she gave up her life in the most ultimate way.

Hashem should grant our entire family and her friends the Heavenly assistance to actively maintain our relationship with Hindy, a"h through greater and greater involvement and dedication to Torah and Mitzvos. Hindy, We love you.

February 13, 2005, Comments at Hindy's Hachnosas Sefer Torah

When Hindy was alive, one of the most frequently made Berachos that we heard from friends was that we should merit bringing Hindy to the Chupah - that she should get married. For years Adina and I dreamed of escorting our sweet beautiful Hindy to the Chupah to get married. This beautiful idea sustained us through very difficult times. But Hashem had other plans, and today in observance of Hindy's Yahrtzeit, we escorted Hindy's sefer torah under the chupah to it's new home in Bais Yaakov, Hindy's school.

Painful Parallels

During Hindy's funeral, I was struck by the fact that the room that we were in to eulogize Hindy was not in a funeral chapel, but rather a banquet hall used for Simchos.

At the cemetery, as I was watching Hindy's casket being lowered into the ground to be buried according to halacha, I was reflecting on what Hindy was wearing therein, white tachrichim - white shrouds. And how I had wished she was wearing a white gown at her Chupah. The searing pain of that moment was unbearable.

For the 1st few days of Shiva, we were worried - how Hindy was/is. Where is she (is she in Gan Eden?), who was she with, was she safe, was she in pain, whose taking care of her?

During the Shiva, I was contemplating how Hindy was free of sin: she was niftar at 17 years of age, and Chazal tell us that a

Grieving & Healing

child who dies less than 20 has no sins *Bain Adom Lamokom* - between her and Hashem. She couldn't have possibly amassed any sins *Bain Adom Lachaveiro* - between her and her friends, since she was hospitalized for the last 2 1/2 years, and the chemotherapy most probably 'burned' away those sins. And think of all of the Tefilos and Chasadim that were done on her behalf to secure her recuperation, that are all deposited in her heavenly bank account for her to cash in - in Olom Haba! Hindy had no sins and the merits of a Tzadekes! She was safe and in Gan Eden! How wonderful it would have been had she achieved this level by living and standing under a Chupah to get married - Chazal tell us that a Chasunah cleanses the sins of the Callah like Yom Kippur does.

And then, with the help of a good friend, Dr. Irving Leibovics, it sort of hit me, like a ton of bricks.

The ultimate chasuna is that of Hashem to Klal Yisroel. The ultimate goal of every Jew is that "yichud" with the Shechina. That is what the Mesilas Yesharim means by "lehisaneg el Hashem"

And perhaps up in Shomayim, Hindy is wearing a white wedding gown and looks beautiful and at peace. There was most probably a simcha going on in the Heavenly Court for Hindy's arrival. All of Hindy's grandparents were there to greet her and welcome her. And Hindy the beautiful Callah must have entered dressed in white, was smiling, had no trouble walking, had no trouble breathing, was in no pain, and was greeted by the Shechina Hakedosha itself.

Hindy was ok, she was in Hashem's hands, and Gan Eden is

exactly where Hashem wants Hindy right now.

In fact, it all now makes sense to me. The previous Shabbos before Hindy was Niftar, at the Malibu Shabbaton, she had celebrated her Shabbos Kalla with all of her friends. Since she had trouble breathing then, her friends were carrying Hindy back and forth from her hotel room to the dining room - as friends carry a Callah at her wedding. In fact, her teacher Chaya Shamie told Hindy on Shabbos that she was so beautiful that she was glowing like a Callah Maidel. And now we were being melaveh her to her chuppa in heaven.

As deep and as great as my sadness was and continues to be that Hindy is not with me, so much more so must be the simchas Adar in Shomayim at the arrival of a such a holy Tsadeikes and her "yichud " with the Kol Yochol.

While Adina and I observed 7 days of shiva it must have been sheva brachos week in the Olam Ha'elyon.

So to you, our good friends, who promised to be first on line to say mazel tov to us at our daughter's wedding, I guess I didn't realize that you already had done so today. I guess you had that Mitzvah Tance with Hindy after all.

And then, with the help of the Yalkut Shemoni it sort of hit me .... again. The Yalkut Shemoni, on Bereishis 20:14 states as follows:

"Reb Yehoshua ben, Levi described Olom Haba: There are two gates made of rubies in Gan Eden, upon which there are six hundred thousand ministering angels whose face shines like the brilliance of the firmament. When a Tzaddik arrives, they remove the garments he wore in the grave and dress him

Grieving & Healing

in eight garments made from the Clouds of Glory. Then they place two crowns upon him, one of precious gems and pearls and the other of gold. Eight branches of myrtle are placed in his hands, while they all praise him and say: "Go eat bread joyfully (Koeheles 9:7). The angels then lead him to a place of flowing rivers. Eight hundred species of rose and myrtle surround this area. *Each person is given a separate chuppa canopy*, as it is written in Yeshayah (4:5) "For in addition to all this honor (there will be) a chuppa.". Four rivers flow there, one flows with milk, another with wine, the third with persimmon, and the fourth with honey. Upon each chuppa there is a golden vine inlaid with thirty lustrous pearls. Each chuppa contains a table made of jewels."

I'm sorry if this all sounds melodramatic, or the rantings of a father who so bitterly misses his daughter, but I just felt I had to share it with you.

"Gevilin Nisrophin Veosyious Porchos Be-Avir"

The tragic story of the death of Reb Chaninah ben Teradyon provided me with an additional powerful visual and a metaphor that helped me cope with Hindy's death.

Reb Chaninah ben Teradyon was a great talmid chochom, a 3rd generation Tanna, who was one of the *"Eser Harugai Malchus,"* one of the 10 holy martyrs whose tragic deaths at the hands of the cruel romans we remember every Tisha Bav and on Yom Kippur.

According to the Gemorah in Avodah Zorah (18), the Romans forbade the learning and teaching of Torah. On the day that Reb Yosi ben Kismah died, on the 27th day of Sivan, Reb Chaninah ben Teradyon was discovered defying the Roman edict and was teaching Torah publically, with a Sefer Torah resting on his lap. The Romans brought him to judgement wrapped in the Torah Scroll, encircled him with bundles of vine shoots, and set him on fire. They ignited him. The Romans then brought tufts of wool, soaked them in water and placed them on Reb Chaninah ben Teradyon's heart, to prolong the burning of his flesh so that his soul not depart his body too quickly.

As the fire raged, Reb Chaninah ben Teradyon's students heard strange crackling noises and saw Reb Chaninah ben Teradyon's eyes watching something rising in the air, and they asked their beloved teacher: "Rebbi, what do you see?" Reb Chaninah ben Teradyon answered them: "*Gevilin Nisrophin Veosyious Porchos Be-avir*" The parchment is burning, but the letters are taking flight to Heaven!

That is, the physical part of the Torah scroll - the parchment - is burning, but the spiritual part - the letters - which impart holiness to the Torah scroll - is soaring to heaven, returning to the source of all holiness.

Considering that Reb Chaninah ben Teradyon was wrapped in the Sefer Torah from which he had been teaching when the Romans had found him, Reb Chaninah ben Teradyon's statement had a double meaning. Both the parchment and his body burned -- true -- but the holy light encased in the letters of the Sefer Torah, along with the holy light that was his soul, flew heavenward, untouched and undamaged by the Roman executioners.

When Hindy died, the concept of Reb Chaninah ben

Grieving & Healing

Teradyon's "Gevilin Nisrophin Veosyious Porchos Be-avir" The parchment is burning, but the letters are taking flight to Heaven! Is what helped me cope with the physical absence of Hindy's body. But while illness destroyed her physical body, Hindy's soul and Neshomah continues to exist and soared to the highest levels where the letters of the Sefer Torah have gone. And when Adina suggested to me that we dedicate a sefer torah in Hindy's memory, it literally took my breath away, for it was the very image of the (burning) Sefer Torah with its letters surviving that provided me with the stark imagery of Hindy's ongoing soul, and it carried me through many a dark moment, and here we are bringing a new sefer torah back into this world in hindy's memory!

That while on Rosh Chodesh Adar one year ago, our Sefer Torah called Chana Hindy was lost, one year later on her Yahrtzeit we are recreating a new Sefer Torah. I began to realize the enormous significance of Hindy's Sefer Torah, and the parallels to Hindy and her memory.

It is taught in a braisa: Rebi Shimon ben Elazar said: Anyone standing by a dead person at the time his soul leaves is obligated to tear Kriah. To what is this likened? To a Sefer Torah that was burned. (Shabbos 105b). In other words, though normally one only tears one's clothing for certain close relatives, being by the person as his or her soul leaves This World is different. It is such a 'tragic' event, like a Sefer Torah being burned, G-d forbid, that all present at the time must likewise rent their clothes. It is an interesting comparison. In a very real sense, the Neshomah inside the body is like the holy letters written on the parchment of a Sefer Torah.

Klausenberg

May 12, 2005, Letter to Rabbi Tzvi Elimelech Halberstam, Sanz Klauzenberger Rebbe of Kiryat Sanz Netanyah

Dear Sanz Klausenberger Rebbe:

Shalom Aleichem. My wife Adina and I lost our 17½ year old daughter Hindy on February 23, 2004, after a 2½ year battle to cancer (Ewings Sarcoma) and during that time and thereafter, we went through the *"Shivah Madurei Gehinom."*

Shabbos Parshas Mishpotim (the Shabbos of Hindy's Yahrtzeit) we were graced with the presence of the Sanz Klausenberger Rebbe in Los Angeles. This was very significant for me because while Hindy was in the Bone Marrow Transport Unit of Children's Hospital, I read her the Feldheim book on the Klausenberger Rebbe's survival of the Holocaust and we were impressed with how he never cracked from his oppression. Hindy & I pledged to each other that we would cite the Klausenberger Rebbe as precedent that no matter what hell we were in the BMT unit, that we would never let it influence / impact our state of mind - and that we pledged to maintain a level of simcha throughout. And we did.

And when Hindy was niftar, the thought of the Klausenberger Rebbe's matzav - as how he lost his wife and 11 children was of significance to me and gave me great chizuk.

At Hindy's first Yahrtzeit, I told the family at the cemetery of a very painful story of the Klausenberger Rebbe in the DP

Grieving & Healing

camp. There was a boy who after the war was turning away from Yiddishkeit, and they brought him to the Klausenberger Rebbe. The Klausenberger Rebbe asked him "You're angry right?" "Well, I lost my wife and 11 children. They took away the best ones and left us. I'm the one that's left." And the Klausenberger Rebbe.took him and embraced him and cried with him and said "They took away the best ones and left us. Kechu Mizimras Haaretz. That's how we have to look at it." And the boy and the rebbe cried. And the boy said later that everyone was speaking to his head. But the rebbe was talking to his heart. Because the Klausenberger Rebbe understood what he felt; that Hashem took the best and left us." ... And this story expresses what I feel: that Hashem took the best - Hindy - and left us.

And of all shabbosim for the Sanz Klausenberger Rebbe to come to our shul, the Sanz Klausenberger Rebbe came, the shabbos of Hindy's yahrtzeit. I was so visibly moved at what you represent. Of the Klausenberger Rebbe who lost everything and rebuilt a family and an empire.

So I'm on a spiritual journey beyond grief trying to cope with Hindy's death, and the aftermath, trying to deal with the pain of losing her. I am wondering if the Sanz Klausenberger Rebbe's father the Klausenberger Rebbe ever spoke of *how* he coped with his tragedies, and *how* he dealt with his pain. It would mean a great thing to me if the Rebbe's written response would be in English.

September 28, 2005, Response from the Sanz Klauzenberger Rebbe of Kiryat Sanz Netanyah, ISRAEL

16 Ellul 5765/ September 2005

Mr. Baruch Cohen

Los Angeles USA

To my esteemed Mr. Cohen:

May you be inscribed and sealed in the Book of Peace, and may all Blessings come to you.

Your letter from the month of June was greatly delayed until I received it, but it seems that one must wait for all good things…

I was extremely moved by your letter. When I read about the personal disaster your family experienced when your beloved daughter passed away, with the pain and distress arising from the page and with which I empathized, I was also quite astounded by your description of how strong her faith had become, as well as your own, and how your complete faith in the Holy One, and which you have fulfilled the commandment as our Sages have explained in Berachot (40b), we are commanded to praise G-d for the bad as we sing His praises for the good we have received.

Such wonderful conduct proves that your daughter was a pure soul who completed its role on earth within a very short amount of time. As my revered father the late Admor (may his memory be a blessing for us) used to teach me, when he explained the Bible section of Shemini with Rashi's explanations, each soul

Grieving & Healing

that comes into this world has a particular and unique mission, a purpose. Each soul has a goal for which it was designated to act and to repair – to make a "TIKKUN" – and each individual does this according to the root of the particular soul, according to its original creation in the Heavenly Throne, and when the soul completes its task, fulfilling its destiny in this world, it returns to its original location, in its original world.

The quotation from Koheleth (1:5) tells us that "The sun rises, and the sun sets- and glides back to where it rises." The goal of the rising sun is to illuminate the earth and its inhabitants, and it is commanded to do so, as described in the Holy Torah. "The sun rises": Just the way the sun shines to fulfill its commanded duty, each Jew conducting oneself honestly and justly is fulfilling the purpose for which the person was created. The root of each person's soul was created with a special purpose, and when that purpose has been concluded, "the sun sets," and the soul returns to its place of origin, "and glides back to where it rises." It strives to return to its place in the Upper World, and although "it glides back to where it rises," as the Sages have said about Moses (Sotah 12b) he still serves G-d.

He added further that the famous words that the Rambam wrote to his son described that "human beings are miserable in this world, in poor and deteriorated conditions, without any rest. Happy is the person who has completed his earthly work, with no more disturbances." Before each Holy Soul comes into this world, like a wanderer far afield from home, into the wilderness, always striving to return home, thus the soul wanders in this world, always seeking to return to its origins. This is also why most newborn babies cry, because the soul weeps to be distanced from its place in the Upper World. This is the implications of "the sun rises." As soon as the baby is born, the soul, always walking in righteous paths, waits until the time of "the sun sets." All of the labor of this world is a burden for the soul, as it strives to "glide back," because the soul knows that instead of being in this world it can be in the Upper World, below the Heavenly Throne, and is in this world not of its own choice, not for its own good. As soon as the soul comes into this world in a newborn baby, it immediately wants to "glide back to its place" because it is shining there, in the Upper Heavenly World, and there is its resting place.

On another opportunity I was lucky to hear from my esteemed late father the Admor explain our requests to G-d during the High Holy Days. We ask for life, we ask "Remember us for life, O King who desires life," we ask to be inscribed in the Book of Life, and other prayers. The revered Admor (may he rest in peace) explained that the entire purpose of human life on earth is to fulfill its G-d given task placed on the soul, to do G-d's will, and, as the Rambam said, happy is the person who can fulfill the mission in a short time, and say goodbye to this world, and go to the next world. This is why we ask G-d "Remember us for life, O King who desires life." Yes, in our life, because in this life we are working "for You, the L-rd of Life," even though I want to 'return home' with all my heart, and find it hard to wait, but while I still must 'repair things' – make TIKUN – in this world, on your behalf, O Living G-d, then I agree that You inscribe me in the Book of Life.

The L-rd's ways are hidden and mysterious and we do not know what is our mission in this world. There was a story about my

Grieving & Healing

late esteemed grandfather, the Tzaddik of Rudnik. There was a chassid who did not have children for a long time, and when a child was born to him, it fell ill after a few months. He was filled with tremendous sorrow and ran to my grandfather, the Rebbe of Sanz, who wrote the Divrei Haim. The chassid wept bitterly, asking the Rebbe to pray for the health of his child. The Divrei Haim went into the room where the baby lay ill, looked at him, and went out. He said to the company that there were those souls who came into this world only to see the countenance of the Tzaddik of that generation…My grandfather z"l the Divrei Haim had barely come back to his home, when messengers came to tell him that the baby had passed away…

There are also stories about The Holy Rebbe Mendele of Rimanov, who had a daughter, whose children all passed away at a young age (G-d spare us). When her tenth son fell ill, she came to her father, weeping and begging him to pray for her son. It was Shabbos, and Rebbe Mendele asked her not to disturb the Sabbath joy. After a while, the boy passed away. Rebbe Mendele began to speak of the greatness of our Father Abraham and ask what was the quality that let him withstand the great trial of being asked to bind Isaac? What made him greater than the thousands of Jews who would have done as G-d asked, or the tens of thousands of Jews who sacrificed their lives because they were Jewish? He explained that Abraham's greatness lay in the fact that when G-d commanded him to take his son, the thought never occurred to him to beg G-d to rescind the evil decree, or ask him not to ask him to sacrifice his only son, but he immediately went joyfully to fulfill the

King's commandment, without a moment of doubt.

We have no idea of these very difficult matters, but we can learn from the stories of our ancestors that the ways of accounting in the Eternal World are very different from considerations in this earthly world, even though in our world we consider such things very sorrowful. It is very praiseworthy that it has been your lot to accept things with joy, similar to how Tzaddikim explained the verse "For you shall go out in joy" as telling us that if you approach things with joy, you can get out of the deepest distress and troubles. This is also the answer to your question as to the power of holding fast to one's faith and religious beliefs held so firmly by my esteemed late father the Admor, despite all of the terrible troubles that he went through. He found the strength because he drew his strength from his wholehearted belief in G-d, and accepted everything that happened to him with joy. I heard from survivors who were together with him during the terrible times of the Holocaust that very frequently they heard him murmuring or saw him moving his lips while reciting the verse, "Because you would not serve the L-rd your G-d in joy and gladness over the abundance of everything" (Deuteronomy 28:47). Of course G-d has given you great merit over your deeds, as the Gemara says (Hagiga 3a) that children come into this world to give reward to those who bring them into this world – their parents. We have seen that children who leave this world have had a purpose for coming into this world - to give merit to their parents.

I am very hopeful that G-d will speedily bring the Moshiach to fill all of us with laughter and joy, that everything will bring blessings, and that G-d will soon bring comfort and

Grieving & Healing

condolences to Zion, and to all of the mourners of Zion and Jerusalem, that you will know no more sorrow, and no more disasters will take place among the Jewish People. Hashem is the great Healer, may He bring healing to all broken hearts and may He order the Destroyer to cease so that His people will only know joy and happiness, with no more sorrow or sighs.

As we approach the New Year, please accept my blessings to you and your family. As the prayerbook says, "May this year end with all its curses," and may you be inscribed in the Book of Peace and Good Life. May the merit of our worthy ancestors protect us, and may you enjoy your children, sustenance and livelihood with complete happiness and constant you. May it be G-d's will.

Rabbi Tzvi Elimelech Halberstam, Sanz-Klausenberg Rebbe

November 30, 2005: Letter to Rabbi Tzvi Elimelech Halberstam the Sanz Klauzenberger Rebbe of Kiryat Sanz Netanyah, ISRAEL

Dear Sanz Klausenberger Rebbe:

Thank you very much for the Rebbe's emotionally heartfelt letter dated 16 Elul 5765. Thank you as well for the great effort of translating it into English. I have read it and reread it several times and it has given me *Nechomah* and *Chizuk*. I have also shared it with my fellow bereaved parents in my *Kehillah* and they have gained from it as well. Thank you.

Carving out *Simcha Mi'Toch Tzarah* is something that I am trying to accomplish. When Hindy's cancer relapsed for the 2nd time, the tumor already encased her entire lungs and her oncologists warned us that she would die a very painful death of strangulation. Rabbonim advised us to sign the DNR - the Directive Not to Resuscitate her in case she went unconscious. We *Davened* to Hashem with all our hearts to have *Rachmonus* on Hindy and spare her from the pain that we feared was in store for her. As her situation became worse and worse, the paramount thought was to relieve her of any suffering. On *Rosh Chodesh Adar*, on the morning of her death, with the blessings of *Daas Torah*, we added a name to her "Ruchomo" in the hopes that Hashem would have compassion on her and on us and take away her *Tzaar*. And He did – that day at 4:33 p.m.. So I thank Hashem for answering our *Tefilos* and returning Hindele's *Neshama* to *Shomayim* quickly. Whenever I feel down, I reflect on Hashem's *Chesed* to us and how He answered our *Tefilos* and feel grateful to Him.

Grieving & Healing

But recently there are times that I find myself so emotionally dead inside that the notion of *Simcha* seems foreign and alien to me. I believe this is due to the fact that Hindy's friends are now getting married and my emotional generator is overheating, and that it's easier for me to shut it down than to feel the pain. To remedy this emotional numbness, I've been learning the *Shaar HaSimcha* of the *Orchos Tzaddikim* and at the advice of a *Chaver*, I started learning HaRav Eliyahu Dessler's *Sefer Michtav Me'Eliyahu* about the concept of *Yeridah Letzoroch Aliyah*, all in the hopes that I can jumpstart my emotional battery and start feeling *Simcha* again. But admittedly, I'm not there yet. Quite frankly, I'm far from it. I still have work to do and I'm hoping that time will heal this wound on some level. I'm hoping that Hashem truly is the healer of the broken hearted).

The Rebbe's amazing letter quotes his father as whispering to himself "*Tachas Asher Lo....B'Simcha*" during the most difficult and trying moments in Auschwitz.

Something amazing happened to me at the time that received the letter that I feel compelled to share. At shalosh seudos of the Shabbos that I received the letter, Rabbi Yaakov Krause - the Morah D'Asrah of Young Israel of Hancock Park spoke and mentioned the fact that the Klausenberger Rebbe ZT"L used to sing the pasuk of "*Tachas Asher Lo....B'Simcha*" during the war. [I almost passed out from the coincidence of receiving the Rebbe's letter that week and hearing Rabbi Krause talk about what the Klausenberger Rebbe whispered to himself to stay strong - all in the same week].

Grieving & Healing

However, Rabbi Krause said it in the following fascinating context: In order to get married in Israel, the Rabbanut has to issue a "marriage license". The process of getting this license involves verifying details about ones Yichus A gentleman who was not frum showed up and the *Bais Din* started to inquire if he is Jewish. His response was of course! The *Bais Din* asked whether he could tell them a Pasuk in our holy Torah? The pasuk he recited was *"Tachas Asher Lo....B'Simcha"* Astounded by the unusual response (usually people would quote *Krias Shma* etc), they asked how he knew that pasuk to which he answered – "my mother was a holocaust survivor and while working in the kitchen she constantly hummed a tune with the aforementioned pasuk. She said the tune was engraved in her mind and on her heart by the Klausenberger Rebbe. She used to watch him in the camps sing this all day and all night."

Grieving & Healing

May 20, 2005, comments to Orthodox Bereaved Parents Support Group in Teaneck, NJ

How are we to understand David Hamelech's statement: *Hofachta Mispedi Lemochil Li* Of transforming mourning into celebration? To be able to sing so beautifully of their life without any recriminations of yesterday's pain? Perhaps the answer and some insight can be derived from the Torah.

Torah the story of the "Song" of the Parshas "Shira." And we all know, that upon witnessing the collapse of the Red Sea drowning the entire Egyptian army, the Torah records the moment in time with the words: '*Az Yashir Moshe*.'

Now the word Shira is a song, in fact, it is the greatest form of simcha and happiness that one can experience. That it, Singing praise to Hashem.

How is it possible that Klal Yisroel could be singing at this particular juncture, at this very difficult moment in time? Especially after what they just went through... Because, In last week's Parshas Bo, we learned that only three days earlier, the majority of the Jewish people died during the plague of darkness, the Makah of Choshech. According to the Meam Loez, four fifths of the Jewish people died during the week of darkness. In all, 600,000 men over the age of 20 survived and left Egypt. Since there were at least 4 women and children for every man, the total number of people living in Egypt prior to the plague of darkness was approximately 13,000,000. From this we see that some 10,400,000 Jews died during the week of darkness. Virtually every family in Klal Yisroel must have

Grieving & Healing

been seriously effected by their own loss of family. They must have been in deep, VERY deep mourning. Yet, we see, that only three days later, Klal Yisroel was …. 'singing' [!?!]. And they were singing a Shirah! Try telling someone who just finished sitting shiva, to go singing … and see what kind of response you will get. How could that be? How can one sing, after losing their family? It sounds superhuman. How is it possible to be singing at that painful point in time?

Rashi observes that the words "Az Yashir Moshe", is written in the future tense: Az Yashir. That Moshe will sing. Perhaps the proper tense should have been past or present tense: Az shaar Moshe - that Moshe sang. Why does the Torah predict and prophesy of what will happen, when it seems to be happening right now?

According to Rashi, 'Az Yashir', is an allusion in the Torah to T'chias HaMeisim…." of that great moment when hashem will bring moshiach, our Messiah, and resurrect the dead.

Perhaps Rashi is teaching us the way to cope with hard times, that one must keep one's focus on the future (i.e., T'chias HaMeisim) and not dwell on the past, in order to conduct a meaningful life, and in order to grow spiritually.

Adopting this prospective attitude is not easy. Perhaps one can try to cope with the physical absence of their loved ones, 'as being temporary.' That if we really believed that Moshiach's arrival is imminent (if we really believed it and not merely engaged in politically correct lip service), and that Techias Hameisim will occur, perhaps it will, and then we would be reunited once again with our loved ones.

Grieving & Healing

So perhaps we should try to convince ourselves on a daily basis: (and my apologies to Paul Revere's 'the British are coming') by insisting that "Moshiach is coming." This way, the physical separation is temporary. By focusing on T'chias HaMeisim, Rashi teaches us, it fills one with hope, rather than dread, and it serves as a salve of sorts to heal and mend the broken heart.

And perhaps the key to how to get to the level of the Az Yashir, perhaps the way to celebrate properly after emerging from hardship is to reflect on the preceding posuk: The Torah says: "Vayaminu Bahashem Uvemoshe Avdo" - That the Jews believed in Hashem and in Moshe Rabbeinu. That their Bitochon and Emunah was immutable and strong. that when a Yid maintains their Bitochon in Hashem, and stays strong during the Makeh of Choshech, when things are dark, and they don't lose his or her belief / Emunah in God, then they will merit and be zoicheh to sing the song of redemption / Geulah and engage in the Az Yashir. That one day the veil separating us will soon disappear, the clouds of tears will part, and there they will be, as beautiful as ever.

March 1, 2006, Chizuk to a group of Chai Lifeline parents

"Never Despair of Hashem's Mercy" adaptions from the Sefer Techias Hameisim by the Biala Rebbe of Lugano Switzerland

"The words of the Sages are blessing. The words of the Sages are wealth.. The words of the Sages are healing." (Kesubos, 103a)

The *Gemarah* in *Berachos* 10a states as follows:

"And it was in those days, that Chizkiyahu HaMelech was sick and dying, and Yishayahu ben Amotz the Prophet came to him and said:

> 'So says Hashem, prepare a will and testament for your house, for you will die, and you will not live."
>
> What is the meaning of the double wording, "You will die, and you will not live?" You will die in this world, and you will not live in the World to Come.
>
> 'Why am I to be punished so severely?' asked the king.
>
> 'Because you did not attempt to father children,' answered the prophet.
>
> 'I refrained from fathering children because I saw through Ruach HaKodesh (Divine Inspiration), that my children would be wicked.'
>
> 'You have no business interfering with Hashem's plans. You must do as you were commanded, and Hashem will do as He pleases.'

Grieving & Healing

'If so, then give me your daughter in marriage, and perhaps through our combined merits, we will have good children,' said the king.

'It is too late. The decree has already been sealed,' said the prophet.

'Son of Amotz! Cease your prophecies and leave! I have a tradition from my father's father (David HaMelech) that even if a sharp sword is held to a person's throat, he must not despair of Hashem's mercy.'"

This concept was expressed elsewhere in a Midrash:

Rebbe Yochanan and Rebbe Eliezer both said that even if a sharp sword is held to a person's throat, he must not despair of Hashem's mercy as the *Possuk* says, "For with the abundance of dreams and many futile things, we must still fear God."

Chizkiyahu HaMelech then turned towards the wall and prayed to Hashem. What is the significance of the wall? Reish Lakish said that he davened from the innermost chambers of his heart, as the *Possuk* says, "My stomach trembles, and the walls of my heart groan."

Rebbe Levi said that Chizkiyahu HaMelech davened concerning the walls of a certain room:

"Master of the Universe, the Shunamite woman built just four small walls to house the prophet Elisha, and in this merit her son was resurrected from the dead. My grandfather (Shlomo HaMelech) built the walls of the Beis HaMikedash and adorned them with silver and gold. In

his merit, let me live."

* * *

I pulled from this amazing *Gemarah* that even when a sharp sword has already begun cutting into a person's throat he should still not despair of Hashem's mercy. We must pay no attention to the discouragements of the doctors trained in secular institutions. We have avenues of healing and deliverance that are unavailable to them.

The *Gemarah* warns that Jews must not endanger themselves by drinking water left exposed, but gentiles are immune from this danger. The *Gemarah* in Avoda Zara 31b says that the laws of *Kashrus* restrict our eating habits, and therefore our bodies work differently from theirs. Furthermore, the constant pressure of observing the many *Mitzvos* of the *Torah* affects our health. Based on these points, the Chasam Sofer writes (Chiddushei Chasam Sofer, Avodah Zara 31b) that the results of medical research conducted on gentiles cannot be applied freely to Jews:

> "In our generation, we have lost the Torah-based tradition of health and healing that was known in earlier traditions. Today, Jewish doctors learn alongside the gentiles in their universities, and are trained using information based on their experience with gentile patients... With regard to maintaining our health, we have no choice but to rely on the opinion of gentile doctors, and place our trust in Hashem that He will plant the correct thoughts in the doctor's mind and the correct words in his mouth. As the *Possuk* says, "Hashem guards the ignorant." When a

Grieving & Healing

gentile doctor tells us that a person's life is at risk, we must trust his opinion and desecrate Shabbos if necessary, in order to save his life. Even if we were to doubt the doctor's credibility, we must act to save a life on the chance that perhaps he is correct. However, with regard to the laws of family purity and secularly-trained doctor's expertise in distinguishing menstrual blood from blood drawn from a wound in the body, what right to we have to trust his opinion? Although the Sages of the Talmud occasionally consulted secular scholars, these Sages understood the Torah's view on biology well enough to accept or reject their opinions as they deemed fit. Today we rely only on their experience with the gentile anatomy, and therefore I am still uncertain how much we can rely on the opinion of doctors in these matters."

The Chazon Ish (Yoreh Deah, Niddah, 99:4) made a similar ruling with regard to the monthly cycles of a gentile woman who converted to Judaism. Although a woman can generally predict the return of her cycle based on the dates of previous occurrences, this is not true of a convert. The pattern of her cycle when she had been a gentile has no *Halachic* relevance once she becomes a Jewess:

> "Purity and impurity have an effect on nature ... Nature is dependent upon mazal and upon a person's awareness of Hashem. Although a woman may have experienced her cycle while she was a gentile, it did not render her ritually impure then. It cannot be assumed that she will experience her cycle on the same day now that she has converted, and, as a Jewess, her cycle now renders her

Grieving & Healing

impure."

We are different from the gentiles, not only in our souls, but also in our bodies. The very matter from which our bodies are formed is substantially different. Therefore, it is clear that the manner of our recovery from illness must also be different. With regard to this, we recite the *Beracha*, "Blessed are You, Hashem, Who heals the sick of His nation Israel."

The Kotzker Rebbe zt"l once said that all despair stems from ignorance. If we truly believe that the body can return from the dead, we must certainly believe that the soul can be revived in a body that still lives. The deepest root of evil is despair; while the principle condition for all worldly or spiritual good is never to despair under any circumstances, but to optimistically look forward for the best. We must pray and labor for our wishes, as if they were small and easily fulfilled. When our prayers are sincere and do not stem from despair, then they will be accepted under any circumstances, even after death.

[Why then, did Chizkiyahu compare himself to the Shunamite's child, who experienced a remarkable miracle and returned from the dead? This was certainly an uncommon occurrence, and should not have been used as a precedent to expect similar miracles in the future.] Perhaps we can now understand why Chizkiyahu HaMelech compared himself to the child who returned from the dead. When Yeshaya prophesied that Chizkiyahu would die, he decreed upon him a sentence of certain death. Chizkiyahu's chances of survival were negligible, like a person with a sharp sword placed at his throat. Even so, he did not despair. He turned to the wall and prayed, that just as the child returned from actual death, he could also recover

Grieving & Healing

from his deathly illness, and defy Yeshaya's prophecy.

Despair is nothing other than a lack of understanding of the true power of prayer. The moment we despair of a loved one's life, we relinquish our hold on him. This is similar to the *Halachah* of returning lost objects found in Bava Metziah 23a: Once the owner has despaired of ever regaining the item, the finder may keep it. So too, when we despair of a loved one's life, we allow the Angel of Death to take him, God forbid. In as far as we are able to speak of such matters, we know that Hashem also observes the laws of the Torah. Just as the Torah prescribes that a lost object must be returned to its owner, as long as the owner has not given up hope of its recovery, so too Hashem will return our loved ones to us, as long as we do not give up hope. In this context, the family and dear friends of the patient are considered like his 'owners' who can demand his return. By praying and exerting our greatest efforts towards their recovery, we show Hashem that we still expect their return.

Prayer that stems from despair has no power. However, if our prayers came from the hope and belief that the patient may yet recover, we could enact the miracle of resurrection through our prayers.

When a person prays but does not truly believe that Hashem can or will help, this is not even considered prayer. The Gemara states that prayer is a service of the heart. Its power comes through the thoughts that move the words. Simply reciting words without believing in them is not a service of the heart. Such prayers are hindered considerably. When we pray with heartfelt sincerity, our ancestors and the *Tzaddikim* who have passed away, awaken and join us in our prayers. However, when we pray with hopelessness and insincerity, they cannot join us. Without their assistance from above, our prayers could never be successful.

Sometimes, we are sent difficulties that seem to have no hope of resolution whatsoever. In truth, these are sent only to help us recognize that we have no one upon whom to rely except Hashem. The test we face is to resist despair, even when it seems that all the gates of prayer have been shut.

April 9, 2006, Hindy's Hatzalah Ambulance Dedication

Morai Verabosai: Last week, Hatzolah issued its official announcement of the Ambulance Dedication in Hindy's memory. Last week was also *Parshas Vayikra* which opens with the *Posuk*: "*Vayikra el Moshe*" Hashem calling out to Moshe. The *Midrash* states:

> "*By your life, the Almighty said, of all your names, I will only call you by the name given to you by Basya the daughter of Pharaoh*" the Egyptian princess.

When Pharaoh's daughter found the Jewish baby floating down the Nile River, she saw the little ark... she opened it, and saw him, a boy weeping! She pitied him, she drew him out of the river and gave him the name "Moshe" (*"Ki Min Hamayim M'sheeseehu"*) "for I have drawn him out of the water."

In fact, the name "Moshe" is the exclusive name that Hashem uses in his communications with the leader of the Jewish people. Nowhere in the Torah do we find explicit reference to any of Moshe's other nine names ("Chaver" "Avigdor" "Tuvia"). Only Moshe.

Rav Shamshon Rafael Hirsch observed that Pharaoh's daughter did not call the baby boy "*Mashui*" - one drawn up from the water. But rather, she called the baby "Moshe" meaning He-Who-Pulls-Others-Out.

Perhaps this gives us an indication of the perspective and Chinuch which the Egyptian Princess gave her foster-son, and of the deep impression that was made from the very beginning

Grieving & Healing

upon his character. By giving him this name "Moshe" she said to him:

> *"All your life, you are never to forget that you were once thrown into the water and that I drew you out of it. Therefore all your life you are to have a soft spot in your heart for other people's troubles and always be on the alert to be a "Moshe", to be a deliverer in times of distress."*

His Hebrew name always kept the consciousness of his origin awake within him. In all this we can see the noble humane character of Moshe's personality.

Perhaps the lesson of today, is that if you, want to be a "Moshe" if you want to be a leader, a savior of others, a Hatzolah member, you have to remember your humble origins: that "from the waters I have drawn him forth" and that "but for the grace of G-d" it could've been me making the Hatzolah call for help. You want to be a "Moshe", you want to save others? Then always remember that you were once a *"Mashui."* Now go save others.

It is very significant that the "name" given to this beautiful ambulance is in memory of our precious daughter Hindy whose pure and holy soul was returned to Hashem two years ago at the tender age of 17. How beautiful is it that Hindy's grandparents chose to forever link Hindy's memory with the special *Zechus* of saving lives.

Our Hindy had a great and very special relationship with her grandparents, her Bubbie and Zaidie: Aba & Mommie: I don't need to tell you how much Hindy loved you. You know. She loved everything about you. Ma: You were the one zoiche to be

Grieving & Healing

with her when her Neshama departed. When Hindy was with her Bubbie she always felt safe and protected. Her beautiful blue eyes always lit up when she was with you. She loved you SO much. We do too. Her final moments on this world were with the Bubby she loves very much. And still loves from Gan Eden. I also do not need to tell you Aba, how much Hindy loved you as well. When her Zaidie was around, Hindy felt safe. You reassured her and made her always feel great. You were her hero.

Adina and I are very grateful and think this is a truly meaningful *Zikaron* for Hindy. It will IY"H save lives and create innumerable *Zechusim* for her precious *Neshama* in *Shomayim*.. *May he swallow up death forever; may Hashem God wipe away tears from every face (Isaiah 25:8).*

T'hei Nishmasa Tzrurah B'tzror Ha'chaim. Thank you.

Grieving & Healing

July 2006, Comments to a Group of Bereaved Parents, Westwood, CA, "If Only We Could See"[2]

Newly married Chaim walked his younger brother David home from shul one Shabbos evening to wish his mother a good Shabbos.

The house glowed with warmth and peace. Candles burned brightly, announcing the arrival of the holy Shabbos. The only thing disturbing the restful atmosphere was the empty chair at the head of the table, the chair that had once been their father's. Since he had gone to his eternal rest two years earlier, longing and anguish filled their hearts.

Their mother sat in her usual place, reading.

"Good Shabbos," her sons greeted her joyfully.

"Good Shabbos," she answered them, trying to hide her tears with a smile.

"Mother! You're crying again," Chaim exclaimed in distress. "Please. Today is Shabbos - crying is forbidden."

"But you know as well as I do," the widow sobbed, "that exactly two years ago today your father left this world! How can I not cry?"

"Yes, Mother," Chaim said kindly, "it is true - today you have a reason. But what about yesterday and the day before? Two years have already passed, and still you are not comforted.

---

2. Inspired by R' Yom Tov Ehrlich, based on the writings of Rav Chaim Vital, the primary student of the great Kabbalist, the Arizal"

Grieving & Healing

You continue to cry and mourn, but do you think this makes Abba happy in Gan Eden? As for our Creator - it is certainly against His Will. The Shulchan Aruch tells us when to mourn and when not to mourn. If you behave differently, you are disobeying Hashem's Will. Forgive me, Mother, for speaking to you this way," Chaim pleaded.

His mother stood up and wiped away her tears. "You are right, Chaim. But, even though I wish with all my heart to forget, I am not able to." She began to sob.

Little Shoshanna begged her, "Mommy, Mommy, we want you to be happy all the time."

"I also want to be happy," her mother whispered. "I promise I will try my best."

Chaim wished his mother "Good Shabbos" and left for his own home. His younger brother, David, made Kiddush over the wine, and the whole family sat down to a wonderful Shabbos meal. A feeling of well-being enveloped the table and everyone felt the true peace of Shabbos. Their mother even laughed. The children told stories from the weekly parasha, and their mother felt so much nachas.

By the time everyone was ready for sleep, it was much later than usual. The widow felt a sense of quiet such as she had not felt since the day her husband left her. She began to think about her fate. She realized, perhaps for the first time, that she was not the only person in her situation. But she also realized that many other young widows had found happiness again, because, unlike her, they had accepted their bitter lot. Her thoughts drifted to the shidduch that had recently been proposed to her. How could she betray her beloved husband's memory! Sleep overcame her, and she dreamt a beautiful dream.

In her dream she saw people running, so she ran too. They all ran out of the city until they came to a thick forest. Even though it was dark, they continued to run. Suddenly, there was a burst of light, and the forest ended.

The sun shone brightly and she saw before her a large garden filled with beautiful flowers which filled the air with a wonderful fragrance. The garden was filled with streams of sparkling blue water. Suddenly, a white-bearded Jew dressed in a long white garment appeared before her eyes. He asked her if she would like to see her husband. Heart pounding, she followed him. The sage stopped near a large tree laden with beautiful ripe fruit. From afar she saw a spacious clearing, surrounded by a golden fence. She saw colorfully dressed Jews sitting in rows learning Torah. In their midst a young man stood teaching them.

"Please wait a moment," said the elderly Jew. "Soon they will conclude the lesson, and you will have a clearer look."

She could not believe the dazzling sights her eyes beheld. When the lesson ended, the teacher began walking towards her. She almost fainted when she saw it was her husband.

"Avraham!" she cried, and swooned against a nearby tree.

"Yes, it is I," her husband replied. "Be calm."

For a tong time, she remained where she was with her eyes closed. When she recovered, she opened her eyes and asked,

Grieving & Healing

"Why did you leave me at such a young age?"

"Please understand," he answered serenely, "that the world in which you live is like a land of exile. People are sent there to complete specified tasks, or to suffer for earlier transgressions. The true world is here. Before you ever knew me, I once inhabited the world below. I was a Torah genius and perfectly righteous. My only fault was that I was unwilling to marry and bring children into the world because I wanted to remain undisturbed in my learning.

"When I departed from that world, I was made head of a yeshiva in Gan Eden, where I began to ascend to ever-higher levels. But when they found out that I had never married and had never had children, I was sent back to the lower world in order to marry and bring children into the world.

So, I married you and, baruch Hashem, we were blessed with children. When our seventh child was born, I was called again to return to my yeshiva in Gan Eden, where everyone awaited me. Great is your merit that I am your husband, for I have a good name here. When the right time will come, we will again live together in this world in delight."

"But," his widow protested, "I did not know you were such a great scholar. You never had much time to learn."

Her husband replied, "I too did not know, since I came to the lower world only to correct what I lacked - that is, to marry and have children, and to provide for them. When I departed from that world, my mind was immediately filled with endless Torah knowledge."

His wife continued her questions. "Why doesn't our Chaim

prosper in his affairs?"

Her husband responded, "You surely remember the din Torah Chaim had with a certain Jew. Although Chaim won legally, he was judged guilty of causing great pain to the other Jew, and faced a harsh sentence. I prayed on his behalf and asked that he be given only four difficult years. In just one more year, the period of his penalty will be complete, and he will begin to prosper."

"And what about our David? Not a single shidduch has been offered him. I don't even have the money to make a wedding."

Her husband smiled and explained: "The reason for that situation is that David's mate was late in coming into the world. She is now only thirteen years old and lives in a distant land. In another five years she will come to your city. She will then become engaged to David and her family will pay for the entire wedding."

His widow began to tremble as a painful memory arose within her. In a soft voice, she asked her husband, "Why was our three-year-old son killed by a drunk?"

Her husband smiled and said, "Follow me!"

She began to walk towards a light-filled garden. Small trees lined her path. Radiant beams of multicolored light shone from above, while beautiful songbirds flew from tree to tree. She found herself able to understand their songs. Some were singing, "Light is planted for the righteous, and joy for the upright in heart." Others were singing, "To sing to Your glory......" She heard: "Peace, peace to the distant and the near......" Small deer leaped back and forth, singing, "I will sing

Grieving & Healing

of Your might; I will laud Your kindness daily." Even the grass was singing: "May Hashem's glory be forever!" The trees too joined in with: "All the trees of the forest will sing."

Suddenly, she saw leaping circles of fire in many colors. They positioned themselves near her in column-like formations, followed by small angels who also settled down near her. A wonderful melody played by musical instruments was heard from all sides, and she felt her soul slipping away. Her husband rushed to place a flower from the garden close to her. Her strength returned, and a chuppa canopy made of sparkling precious stones appeared before her. Under the canopy facing her stood a small angelic form. She recognized her murdered son, who was now laughing with great joy. Again she felt faint, and again her husband gave her the flower to smell. She opened her eyes, and saw that she was not mistaken - it really was her son.

"Why did you leave me when you were so young?" she asked.

"Everything is in accordance with the plans of the Creator," he answered, "I had already been in the world once before, as a member of a prominent family. There had been wild attacks on the Jews in our town, and the gentiles murdered everyone. I was the only survivor. I was then about six months old and a gentile woman took me in to her house and raised me, until I was redeemed by Jews. They taught me Torah and I studied until I became a great Torah scholar. I lived the rest of my life in comfort and peace. When I left that world, I was received in the True World with joy. I rose higher and higher, until I reached a point where I could rise no higher because I had nursed from a non-Jewish woman. It was decreed that I be born again to a Jewish mother, and live those early years in purity. That way, I would be able to continue to rise in the upper world.

"I was then born to you, Mother. It was a great merit for you. After three years I was taken back to my place, for there was nothing left for me to do in that lowly world."

"But why were you taken in such a horrible way?" his mother asked.

"When I was about to depart from the world," explained her son, "a terrible decree was issued against the Jews of our town - everyone would have died, including you and Abba. I was given the honor to be the sacrifice for the entire town. I was killed for their sake, and thus the town was spared. For that reason I receive all this honor now. Nobody in Gan Eden is allowed to approach me except for Abba, who can see me whenever he wishes." The child laughed softly, and wandered away until he disappeared from view.

"So you see now - there is an answer to all your questions," the Torah scholar told his wife. "Our Creator does no evil."

"I must return now to my students," be concluded. He escorted her to the place where she had first opened her eyes, near the great tree, where he said to her: "It is very good here, but I cannot bear to see your suffering. You will do me a great favor if you now begin to live happily. You have been offered a shidduch - please accept it."

He vanished, and once again the old man appeared and led her back to the forest.

Grieving & Healing

She awoke from her dream a changed person. For a long time she lay in her bed with a smile on her face, as the images of her content husband and smiling son lingered in her mind. A great stone had been lifted from her heart, and she was consoled.

She remarried, and lived a life of happiness and contentment.

The Ari z"l taught deep secrets of the Torah and, in particular, the subject of gilgulim, transmigration of souls. He taught that all creatures are like cogs in the great machine called Creation. HaKadosh Baruch Hu places each cog in the world and adjusts it to suit the operating needs of the mechanism. He brings into the world souls that have a function in this world, and removes the souls that are needed Above, for this world and the Next World are both part of the same machine.

Here below, the machine operates with souls plus bodies, while Above, it works with souls alone. If we would know how it all works, we would never become upset, for in the very near future, all the souls will return to this lower world. Here, they will serve Hashem with body and soul combined, until all the physical bodies will become purified and soul-like. This last stage will take place towards the end of the sixth millennium, which will be followed by the "Great Shabbos" (R. Chaim Vital, who heard it from his great teacher the Ari z"l).

Grieving & Healing

February 2007, Hindy's 3rd Yahrtzeit Seudah

Miriam's Rebuke to Amram

"One year before Moshe was to be born, Moshe's father Amram divorced his wife Yocheved. Because Amram and Yocheved were the two leading Jewish personalities, the Jews followed their lead and divorced their spouses. This was done in response to Pharaoh's decree to "drown all male children".

The Talmud (Sotah 12b) explains Amram's reasoning. "Are we to labor at having and raising children for nothing"? He therefore divorced his wife in hope of guaranteeing that no other male children would be born. Miriam, their 5 year old daughter, disagreed with her father's reasoning. "Dad, your decree is more severe than Pharaoh's! Pharaoh only decreed against the male newborn, your decree extends to all children, both male and female! Pharaoh's decree is only against souls living in this world, but at least the child is born, is killed, and his soul goes directly to the World to Come; but your decree guarantees that souls won't even have a chance of attaining the World to Come! Being that Pharaoh is an evil man, there is no guarantee that G-d will allow his decree to be fulfilled; but you father are a Tzadik, and Hashem always fulfills the decrees of His Tzadikim! The Talmud concludes that Amram listened to Miriam's arguments and remarried Yocheved. Once Amram remarried his wife, the rest of the Jews also remarried their wives and resumed having children. It was a result of Amram's and Yocheved's second marriage that Moshe, the redeemer,

Grieving & Healing

was conceived and born."

It occurred to me how powerful her words could be, when viewed through the prism of a bereaved parent like myself. One of the byproducts of this painful and bitter Nisoyon of losing a child, is that my entire perspective on life and Torah changed dramatically, in that I pick up on different ideas that I never even noticed before. I see things very differently. It's as if I'm in a different universe; and breathe a different oxygen. I've heard this exchange between Miriam and Amram for years. But now that I lost Hindy, I hear a very different message emanating from it. If I understand Miriam's 2nd argument to Amram (in bold below): it would have been better for these souls to be born in Olam Hazeh -- even to die subsequent and brutal deaths by drowning in the Yam Suf -- even to die shortly after birth -- just to merit entry into Olam Haba! That a "Ben Olam Haba" qualifies by living on earth for any period of time, and that brief and tortured life is far better for the Neshomah than not to have been born at all because it is the key that opens the door for entry to Olam Haba. I find this concept to be of significant Nechomah to any parent who has lost a child.

The Dubno Maggid's Moshol of Naive City Boys & Bread

There were two simple brothers who were reared in the city and had never stepped oUt of the confines of the city to visit the countryside. They were also quite naive and unschooled in agricultural matters. One day they decided to visit the country and came across a beautiful, lush, and smooth piece of land. While they were admiring this expensive piece of real estate, along came a man (a farmer) and began to plough the field, turning it into a mass of shallow rough ditches.

"Hey, do you see what sort of crazy people they have here in the country?" said one brother to the other. "They purposely ruin a beautiful and expensive piece of land for absolutely no reason." "Let's be patient and wait a while and see what's going to happen," replied the other brother. "Perhaps there is a reason why he did that."

The next day they returned to the field just in time to see the farmer empty some sacks of good wholesome grain into the narrow ditches (furrows) that he had dug the day before. "I don't believe my eyes," said the skeptical brother. "Did you see what he just did? He took good food and wasted it; he threw it on the ground and covered it with earth. I'm going back to the city where the people are normal. If we stay around here any longer we may become influenced by their meshugene country behavior."

So he went home. But the other brother, a little more trusting of the country folk, decided to stick around to follow up the curious ways of the farmer. Perhaps after all, there was a method to the madness. The remaining brother visited the field every day and as time went by he noticed straight rows of green stalks sprouting up from all of the furrows. "So that's what it's all about," he said to himself. "The grain that the farmer threw into the ground produced these beautiful plants. That's amazing!"

He quickly phoned his skeptical brother, who had returned to the city, and told him that he must come back to the country

Grieving & Healing

immediately. "You won't believe what happened," he said. "The farmer was not so crazy after all. Come back and you'll see why he ruined the land and the grain!"

Well, what do you think happened on the day the brother from the city joined his brother in the country? Just on the day that he arrived and as he was showing his brother the field with the beautiful plants that had grown out of the "ditches" and were now in full bloom, along came the farmer with his reaper and chopped down all the plants (shoots of grain). What was before a beautiful field with orderly rows of lovely plants had turned into a disorderly mess, a scene of wilfull destruction and wanton waste.

The two brothers stared at the field in horrified shock. "Is this what you called me back for?" asked the skeptic of his brother. "Did you want to subject me to viewing more madness? You are a fool for being so trusting. Come back with me now, before you turn crazy, too."

But the trusting brother decided to wait. He watched patiently as the farmer bound the fallen stalks into bundles. He watched as he threshed the bundles, separating the straw from the kernels and the kernels from the chaff. He watched as the kernels were piled high, loaded into a wagon, and taken to the mill. For a moment, after the grinding, he was disappointed to see that the kernels had been turned into a white powdery dust. "Again you have destroyed," he thought to himself. But he was beginning to see that obviously there was some pattern of activity that was going on. So he decided to be patient and follow the pattern to the very end, so he obtained permission from the farmer to accompany him and watch everything that ensued.

The farmer put the powder (flour) in sacks, took them home, and mixed the flour with water. The brother was puzzled with the "whitish mud," but knew that something exciting was about to happen that would unravel the entire mystery. Sure enough, the farmer fashioned the "mud" into a square-shaped loaf, put the loaf in the oven, and waited. Finally he opened the oven and a tantalizing aroma wafted through the air. The brother couldn't believe his eyes. There in the farmer's hand was a freshly baked crisp brown bread, better than any bread the brother had ever seen on his kitchen table in the civilized and normal city where he lived.

As they savored together the delicious bread, the farmer turned to the trusting brother. "Now," he said, "now you understand!"

We are like naive city boys who descend on this earth, God's country try, for a few years and are confronted with what seem to us to be some very strange and incomprehensible sights. But the Almighty has a divine plan for the world that can span six thousand years. We only see disjointed fragments of that plan. We cannot follow the process from beginning to end. But we must be patient and trusting, having faith that every thing even that which seems tragic, painful, and destructive-is part of an ultimate Divine plan that will create an end goal of beauty, happiness, fulfillment, and eternal reward.

The Two Ships of Koheles Rabah

Rabbi Pinchas said, . . . When a child is born all are happy; when a man dies all are sad. But it should not be that way. For when a person is born one should not yet rejoice for one does

Grieving & Healing

not know what his actions will be, righteous or wicked, good or bad. But when he dies, there should be gladness over the fact that he passed away from this world with a good name and departed this world in peace. This can be compared to two ships that crossed on the high seas. One was just leaving the port; the other was returning. All were happy to send off the one that was departing; the one that was returning did not stir too much rejoicing. There was a wise man there who exclaimed, "It should be just the opposite. There should be no rejoicing over the ship that just left the port for no one yet knows how it will fare. How many rough seas will it encounter? How many accidents may occur to it? But over the one that is entering all should rejoice, because we see it has returned in peace."

So it should be with the human being. When a man dies we can be glad and full of praise that he departed this world with a good name and in peace. This is what King Solomon meant when he said, "And the day of his death [is better] than the day of his birth."

Finding the Word "Nechamah" in the Torah

At the end of *Parashas Bereshis*, before the Flood, when Hashem sees that mankind is wicked, the *Pasuk* states (6:6): "*Vayinachem Hashem Ki Asah Es Ha'adem Ba'aretz, Vayitatzev El Libo,* And Hashem has comforted that he made man on earth, and He grieved in his heart." What can he possibly mean? What kind of *nechamah* could Hashem have had *before* the Flood? Rashi explains: *The thoughts of Hashem turned from the attribute of mercy to the attribute of justice... He reconsidered what to do with man, and similarly, wherever the Torah uses the term* nechamah, *it means to reconsider what to do.* Nechamah does not mean to forget and move on. It does not even mean that we stop grieving. Thus, the end of the *pasuk* states, "*Vayitatzev el libo.* And Hashem grieved in his heart." Even though He had *nechamah,* he continued to grieve. Even after His "change of heart." His heart was still struggling. *Nechama* means to reconsider what was originally thought, to reevaluate the situation. At Hindy's funeral, we thought that we could not go on without Hindy, and that we'd never be happy again. Now we have learned that we must.

"Rav Lach Sheves Be'emek Habocho"

Every Friday night, when I make Kiddush Friday nights, I think of Hindy and mentally try to include her in my Kiddush. When I bentsch my children on Friday nights before Kiddush, I'm mentally bentsching Hindy as well. She's still my daughter, I'm still her father, I still love her and still care for her welfare.

Notwithstanding my efforts to elevate my Neshomah with hers, and to connect with her, this past Friday night I was missing Hindy terribly, and I was seized with tremendous pains of separation, crying uncontrollably during Kabolas Shabbos (I wished I had a tallis over my head). At some point in time, I regained my composure as the Chazzan Yaakov Rosenblatt was singing Lecha Dodi: *"Rav Lach Sheves Be'Emek Habocho, Vehu Yachamol Alayich Chemla."* Too long have you dwelled in the Valley of Tears.

For a second, I thought that a Navi with Ruach Hakodesh observed my pain and placed his hand on my shoulder and

Grieving & Healing

said: 'Rav Loch Sheves Be'Emek Habocho'" you've cried for too long in the valley of tears, and the time has come to 'move on.' Never forget Hindy, but we need to move on. And if you are wondering how you will have the werewithall to pull yourself out of the thicket, rest assured that "*Vehu Yachmol Aliach Chemlah*" that the RBSO will comfort you because He is the *Rofeh Lishburei Lev* and will heal your broken heart over Hindy. I got nechomah for a moment, at that moment, dried my tears and proceeded to be happy on Shabbos.

"Gezeirah Al Hameis Shenishtakech Min Halev"

I want to share with you a Diyuk and an original Machshoveh. When the Torah states that Yaakov Avinu refused to be consoled by Yosef's brothers and sisters over Yosef's violent death by wild animals, Rashi explains that "*Gezeirah al hameis shenishtakech min halev*," The Diyuk is: that the dead are Nistakach min 'Haleiv' but not min 'HaRosh' - that the dead are forgotten from the heart, but not from the mind, just like you said about Rabbi Bulka. I looked up the source of the Gemorah in Pesachim for the Gezeirah and from the gist of the idea, it would be expected that the phrase read that the Gezeirah should be on the mourner's heart, that the deceased be forgotten. However, it appears from the sentence structure of the Gezeirah, that the subject of the Gezeirah is 'al Hameis' - that the decree is on the dead. I wrestled with this a bit. Maybe there is indeed a decree on the dead. Maybe there is a Chesed to the deceased, that allows them to truly enjoy Gan Eden and not be burdened by traces of this world, because they truly now know by virtue of the decree that their families are moving on,

89

that they are no longer paralyzed from the crushing effects of grief, that they are not grieving excessively, and that Shikchah has kicked in on some level.

June 2007, BYLA Graduation, Presentation of Hindy Cohen Middos Award

I'd like to share with you a beautiful *Machshovah* that is relevant to our awardee, is relevant to Hindy, and is, in fact: "vintage Hindy" for those of you who were fortunate enough to have known her. This comes from the Biala Rebbe of Lugano Switzerland / a powerful observation indeed. Shulchan Aruch provides that Mishenichnas Adar *Marbim* BeSimcha, Mishenichnas Av *MiMaatim* BeSimcha. Notice how it doesn't say that when the month of Av comes we increase our tears, or we increase our sadness, or we increase our misery, but rather, the Shulchan Aruch says to *lessen* our Simcha. That it's not about whether or not to be BeSimcha, it's *how much* Simcha we generate. That the constant in our lives must be Simcha. The pilot light to our stove-tops, must always be "on." Again, the constant in our lives must be Simcha. Some months its magnified, and some months its decreased. But one always has to be BeSimcha. Before Pesach ... Tali interview en route to Israel we asked Tali: "What character trait best exemplifies you? Tali: "Aba, it's being BeSimcha" When asked why this *Midah Tovah* best personifies Tali, she replied that this is a beautiful way for her to maintain her connection with Hindy ... to always be BeSimcha. So you can understand the *Chashivus* of this beautiful *Machshoveh*, it's relevance, the enormity of this moment, and the beauty of being BeSimcha, with Hindy, with Tali, and our awardee.

March 16, 2008, Comments at Mesivta of Greater Los Angeles School Trustee's Dinner

Morai Verabosai: Nine days ago, on Erev Shabbos, Friday March 7, 2008, I received a phone call from Rabbi Shlomo Gottesman informing me of the good news of the birth of his grandson, and "by the waywould you like to MC our banquet." The truth of the matter is that these 9 days have been hectic for me, with a 4-day trip to NY, a 2-day trial, and my hosting the Kosover Rebbe at my home. Who had time to prepare one's thoughts to MC properly? I told Rabbi Gottesman, "yes" instinctively, that I would be happy to MC, that I could not say no to him. And "by the way, Rabbi Gottesman, mazal tov on your grandson." May you and your wife see a lot of Naches from Chaim Yitzchok. That day that he called was Rosh Chodesh Adar II and was the 4th Yahrtzeit of my daughter Hindy. So in the further merit of Hindy's Neshamah, I had another good reason to say yes to Rabbi Gottesman, in honor of the great friendship and closeness that I feel towards him, and in honor of the great Chavreusashafh that we once had, that I miss very much.

But being that Rabbi Gottesman has given me this platform in which to serve as an MC, for a beautiful Torah Kehillah, celebrating Torah in CA, I feel a certain Achrayus to pause, before we celebrate, and comment about the times that we find ourselves in difficult times. Painful times. How can we think of Adar and how can we think of being BeSimcha, when tragedies surround us. When our friends suffer the loss of a daughter and granddaughter in one felt swoop, in one car crash.

Grieving & Healing

Mercaz HaRav Tragedy

Can mere words describe the magnitude of the tragedy across the world in Yerushalayim at Yeshiva Mercaz HaRav Kook? The outpouring of grief, the pure *Yiddishe Tzaar*, the tears and the anguish were so powerful and tragic that no person with a heart could remain unmoved.

No person at that tragic levaya of eight innocent *Bochurim* could return to mundane, everyday life. None of the attendees could return home to eat lunch, read the paper, or even engage in the pursuit of parnassa. All felt the instinctive pull to bury their tear-stained faces in a Gemara, in a Tehillim, or anything that could invoke Divine mercy and beg Hashem, *"Mi she'omar l'olamo dai, yomar litzaroseinu dai."* For those not at the levaya, just the media pictures of eight figures wrapped in *Tachrichim* lined up next to each other were heartbreaking. And as *Ehrliche Yidden*, we have an obligation to Be *Noseh B'ol*, to share the burden of tragedy with those directly affected.

Just think of the parents, the fathers and mothers of these bochurim, who raised these children from infancy, merited to watch them grow and blossom, and sent them to learn in yeshiva Human nature is such that, rightfully or not, we will eventually move on and forget about this tragedy. The parents won't. The pain that is their lot and will continue to be their lot is something that we, as Jews, are obligated to feel.

Their pain should be our pain. Their tragedy is our tragedy. It is the most elementary duty of being *Noseh B'ol Im Chaveiro*. It's the mark of a Yid.

The Klausenberger Rebbe's Insight

I think it is worthwhile to quote the previous Klausenberger Rebbe zt"l from a Chumash-Rashi shiur said in 1984. The Klausenberger Rebbe offered practical advice on what believing Jews should do in such terrible situations, advice that seems as current today as when he gave it 25 years ago. *"We must strengthen ourselves in emunah and understand that two things are completely above and beyond the normal order of nature. One is the terrible Jew hatred and wickedness that has gripped the Arabs. The second is the power of our emunah and yiras Shomayim, an emunah and yiras Shomayim that invests in us the ability to completely distance ourselves from having anything to do with these wicked people."* Let us not be swayed by the words of 'experts,' 'professors,' and secular journalists who constantly spew venomous hatred of our holy Torah [while advocating suicidal "cooperation with the Arabs]..." "Tayereh Yidden - Dear Jews, let us come together, let us not be afraid of the ever strengthening powers of wickedness that seek to prevail. Let us grab onto the Holy Torah and simple emunah. Only then will Hashem help us."

What powerful moving and relevant words to us then, and to us now. And I know that this is a Trustee's banquet, and the mood has to be upbeat, and it is, but when something this tragic to Klal Yisroel weighs so heavily on our hearts, we must acknowledge it, connect with our brothers and sisters in Eretz Yisroel, and not merely numb ourselves and try to forget their cries.

Grieving & Healing

June 2008, BYLA Graduation, Presentation of Hindy Cohen Middos Award

"Mishenichnas Adar Marbim B'simcha"

Hindy was *Niftar* on Rosh Chodesh Adar II - 5 years ago. The *Halacha* states that: "*Mishenichnas Adar Marbim B'simcha*" - When the month of Adar *enters*, we increase in joy." Interesting word choice. Instead of *mishenichnas* (when the month enters), it might have said, *Kisheba* (when the month Adar arrives). The saintly *Sfas Emes* derived from this that we can only feel joy, when we permit the joy to enter ourselves. We must open our hearts to feel the joy of an occasion. We must allow the joy to enter. One who allows the joyous month of Adar to enter within, will be able to experience happiness again, despite the loss s/he experienced.

What are we welcoming when we allow Adar *to enter*? Wherein lies the abundance of joy, that comes into the world with the month of Adar? And the answer is *Change*. Adar is *Hachodesh Asher Nehepach*, the month that can change, *Miyagon L'simcha*, from sadness to joy, *May'aivel L'yom Tov*, from mourning to celebration.

The powerful metaphor of the Shattered Luchos[3]

There is a precedent for this concept with the *Luchos*. Moshe Rabbeinu broke the first set of *Luchos* on one of the saddest days of the Jewish Year. But there was another, permanent set

---

3. Inspired by Rebbetzin Esther Yungreis

of *Luchos* that came afterwards. When we feel that our "set of *Luchos*" are shattered, we need only open our hearts to receive Hashem's gift of a "second set of *Luchos*," the belief that joy can, and will, find a place in our lives again, with *Luchos* that will never be broken.

But there's more: Which is why the Chachamim tell us that not only the whole Luchos, but also the broken ones, were situated in the Kodesh Kodoshim. This conveyed the message articulated at the very genesis of Judaism: From the broken pieces of life you can create a holy of holies.

Hashem affirmed Moshe Rabbeinu' decision to break the Luchos. Hashem told him, "Thank you for breaking them." Because the broken Luchos, representing the shattered pieces of human existence, have their own story to tell; they contain a light all their own. Truth is found not only in wholesomeness, but also—sometimes primarily—in the broken fragments of the human spirit There are moments when Hashem desires that we connect to Him as wholesome people, with clarity and a sense of fullness; there are yet deeper moments when He desires that we find Him in the shattered experiences of our lives.

We hope and pray to always enjoy the "whole tablets," but when we encounter the broken ones, we ought not to run from them or become dejected by them; with tenderness we ought to embrace them and bring them into our "holy of holies".

I'm sure you appreciate the enormity of this powerful metaphor of the *Shattered Luchos* and its applicability.

Shlomo Hamelech wrote in Shir Hashirim: - My Beloved (Hashem) stretched His hand out through the pit and my

Grieving & Healing

insides were churning for Him;- and I got up to open the door for my Beloved.

Even as a young child, the Kotzker Rebbe was well known for his sharp wit. A visiting Rabbi, approached the small boy, "So Menachem Mendel," he challenged, "Tell me, where is Hashem? Without missing a beat, the boy responded, "Hashem is wherever you let Him in."

The Cohen family and BYLA have all experienced a *shvira*, a shattering, with Hindy's death, that left a gaping hole in its wake, a hole that can never completely disappear.

How do we avoid stumbling over that hole? How do we begin to welcome joy into our lives with the belief in a "new set of *Luchos*"?

Obviously, only the Infinite One - *Hashem Yisorach* - can fill an infinite hole. "*Dodi shalach yado min hachor* - Our Beloved One reaches His hand out from the pit." But He, must be beloved by us, He, must be familiar by us, and, as the young Kotzker so wisely noted, we, must actually get up and open the door for Him. Hashem extends his hand in love, in support. He is there for us. But only if we allow Him access. And hence, the word: "*Mishenichnas*." As it states in Shir Hashirim: "*Kamti ani lifto'ach l'dodi*" - only if we open the door to let our beloved, *Hakadosh Baruch Hu*, in, can we experience joy.

Inviting *Hashem* in, to our lives, building a strong relationship with Him - at any time, in any language - not only injects meaning into our lives, but it also leaves space for *Hashem*, to fill the seemingly endless, bottomless cavities that remain after a *Petirah*.

We will never forget Hindy. We always think about her, but we continue on, with the "second set of *Luchos*" even after our first set was broken and shattered.

So you can understand the *Chashivus* of this beautiful *Machshoveh*, it's relevance, the enormity of this moment, of how important it is to us that you at BYLA remember Hindy, in a proper *Bakovodicker* way.

May 1, 2009, Halacha's Sensitivity to Bereaved Parents – the Halachic Prohibition of Kissing a Child in Shul During Davening

This Shabbos morning, I learned something that validated my "Agmas Nefesh" - grief everytime I'm in shul and I see a father kissing his children in shul. It has caused me pain ever since Hindy died. I kept wondering why parents do it; weren't they self-conscious that I'm sitting right next to them and see this and feeling horrible?

The Sefer "Veharev Nah", of the Torah of Harav Yitzchok Zilberstein in Parshas VaEschanan (enclosed), cites a "Sefer Chassidim" that was written by Reb Yehuda HaChassid (4910-4977; 1150-1217) that: (1) one should not kiss one's children in shul when one is sitting next to a married person who has no children so as not to cause the barren person Agmas Nefesh (# Tof Resh Lamed Tes); & (2) one should not walk with one's children near a person who's (only) child died so as not to cause the bereaved parent to remember his Agmas Nefesh (# Tof Resh Mem).

I instinctively knew that it caused me pain to see a father's affection for his child in shul, but couldn't put my finger on the Torah-based source that it was insensitive to those who have buried children. The Halacha is that one should not show affection to children in shul because one should reserve their affection for Hashem in Shul. That I knew. But I was searching for validation as to the insensitivity factor and now I found it and the source. According to the Sefer Chassidim, seeing other families intact, with displays of affection, causes us aggravation and pain. Wondering if Reb Yehuda HaChassid was a bereaved parent to have such sensitivity.

May 2009, Comments to a group of Orthodox Jewish Bereaved Parents

Perspectives on Life in the World to Come; Through the Brilliant Prism of the Gesher Hachaim[4]

Shlomo Hamelech taught us in Koheles 7:2 that *"it is better to go to the house of mourning than go to the house of partying, for it [death] is the end of all mankind, and the living will attend their hearts to it."* Two verses later, Shlomo Hamelech teaches us in *Koheles* 7:4 that *"the heart of the wise is in the house of mourning, the heart of the fool is in the house of rejoicing."*

The wisdom of King Solomon applies to *all* people. It takes into consideration any and every one. It takes into account all of the reasons and rationalizations for avoiding a visit to the house of mourning. The statements are clear. It is wise and proper for anyone to pay a condolence call. We will examine briefly this wisdom.

An incredible story is told in Sefer Histaklus Hanefesh, of the great chassidic master Reb Simcha Bunem of Przysucha. During the final moments of his life, as he lay on his death-bed, his wife, seeing the end drawing near and unable to control her grief, burst into tears. Immediately he turned to her and said, "Why are you crying? All my life was only that I should learn how to die!" And with these words, with a radiant smile upon his face, he returned his soul peacefully to his Maker.

It is true that the Zohar in *Parshas Vayechi* 223b tells us that

---
4. Inspired by Rabbi Aaron Levine

Grieving & Healing

no man can ever contemplate his own death. "*Rabbi Elazar said that even were a man to live a thousand years, on the day that he departs from this world it seems to him as though he had existed for one day.*" As long as the soul is joined to the body, as long as we live on this earth, the urge to live is so powerful that we cannot come to grips with our own death, our separation from the life of the body. The *Mishnah* in *Pirkei Avos* 4;22 says "*Against your wish you shall die.*" No one wants to die. But it is the inescapable eventuality of every human being. As the *Gemorah* in *Kesuvos* 8b says, "*Our brethren who are worn out and crushed by this bereavement, set your heart to consider this; This [death] stands forever; it is a path from the six days of Creation. Many have drunk, many will drink [from the Cup of Sorrow] ... Our Brethren, the Master of Consolation should comfort you. As it says in Sefer Bereishis 3:19: "From dust we came and to dust we shall return.*"

Life on this earth is transient; it is only the corridor to a greater life in the World to Come. As it says in the *Mishnah* in *Pirkei Avos* 4:16: "*Prepare yourself in the anteroom so that you can enter the palatial hall of the World to Come.*"

Insights of the Gesher Hachaim

Although the notion of life in the World to Come is foreign to us, the great scholar HaRav Yechiel Michel Tuchachinsky, who died in 1955, offered us a parable in his magnum opus "*Sefer Gesher Hachaim*" that draws us closer to an understanding of the reality of life in the World to Come. His analogy is starkly dramatic, conveying the belief in the reality of the Afterlife even though this must be refracted through the prism of death. What

Grieving & Healing

follows is an adaptation of the parable as developed by Rabbi Maurice Lamm in his masterpiece entitled: "*Consolation: The Spiritual Journey Beyond Grief*" 2004 © Rabbi Maurice Lamm, Jewish Historical Press:

Imagine twin babies growing peacefully in the warmth and safety of their mother's womb. Their lives are secure and all of their needs are met. Their whole world is the interior of the womb. They cannot conceive of another world - one larger, better, and more comfortable that the one in which they presently live. As they drop lower and lower down the birth canal, they begin to wonder, "Surely if this continues we will one day cease to exist here. Then what will happen to us?"

Now the first infant is a believer. He is heir to a tradition that tells him that there will be a "new life" after this wet, warm existence of the womb - a strange belief, seemingly without foundation, but one to which he clings steadfastly. The second infant is a complete skeptic. Mere stories do not convince him. He believes only in that which can be clearly demonstrated. He is enlightened and tolerates no idle conjecture. What is not within one's experience can have no basis on one's imagination.

Says the believer: "After our 'death' here, there will be a great, new world. We will eat through our mouths, we will see great distances, we will hear through our ears, our feet will be straightened, our heads up and free - rather than down and bent over."

"Nonsense," replies the skeptic. "You're straining your

imagination again. There is absolutely no foundation for this belief. It is a historically conditioned subterfuge, an elaborate defense mechanism designed to calm your fear of 'death.' There is only this world. There is no world to come."

"Well, then" asks the first, "what do you think it will be like?"

The second brother snappily replies with all of the assurances of the slightly knowledgeable, "we will go with a bang. Our world will collapse and we will sink into oblivion. No more. Nothing. Black void. An end to consciousness. Forgotten." These may not be comforting thoughts, but they are reasonable ones.

Suddenly the water inside the womb bursts and the womb convulses. Upheaval, turmoil, writhing - everything lets loose. Then a mysterious pounding - faster, faster, lower, lower. The believing brother, tearing himself from the womb, exits and falls outward. The skeptic in the womb hears an ear-splitting cry and a great tumult from the black abyss. He shrieks, startled by the 'accident' that befell his brother. He bewails the tragedy, the 'death' of his perfectly healthy brother. "Why didn't he take better care of himself; why did he fall into that terrible abyss? Oh, what a horrible end, just as I predicted!"

Meanwhile, as the skeptical brother mourns, his 'dead' brother has been born into the 'new world.' The ear-splitting cry is a sign of health and vigor and the tumult of the chorus of mazal tovs sounded by the waiting family, thanking G-d for the birth of a healthy son.

Grieving & Healing

Says Rabbi Tuchachinsky: "Just as we separate and 'die' from the womb, only to be born into a better life, so too, we separate and die from our earthly world, only to be reborn to a better life of eternity. The exit from the womb is the birth of the baby. The exit from the body is the re-emergence of the soul at a higher level. Just as the womb requires a gestation period of 9 months, so too, this world requires a residence period of some time. As the womb is a corridor to life in this world, this world is a corridor to eternal life in the World to Come."

Rabbi Abie Rotenberg's Conversation in The Womb

In fact, Rabbi Abie Rotenberg captured this amazing parable in a beautiful song in Journeys I, entitled, *"Conversation in The Womb"*:

> *My dear brother, look around and tell me what your eyes behold.*
>
> *Don't deny that you see, it's only you and me, and our existence*
>
> *It is empty, it is cold; our existence it is empty, it is cold.*
>
> *But dear brother, you must have faith that we are not the only ones*
>
> *Because in the distance there is a place, where we'll stand up tall and straight*
>
> *Oh, I believe that there is a world to come*
>
> *Yes, I believe that there is a world to come.*
>
> *My dear brother, don't be blind, don't be stubborn, don't*

be set.

Imagination, it's all right but it won't light up the night.

What you see is exactly what you get, what you see is exactly what you get.

But dear brother, you will surely find when all is said and done

That the future it will show there is so much we don't know.

Oh, I believe that there is a world to come

Yes, I believe that there is a world to come.

My dear brother, where have you gone, is this the moment I have known?

I can faintly hear the cry, my dear brother must have died, it's all over

Now forever I'm alone, it's all over now forever I'm alone.

But dear brother, please don't mourn me when my life has just begun.

What you are hear are sounds of joy, congratulations it's a boy.

Soon you'll be here with me in this world to come

Soon you'll be here with me in this world to come

Midrash Tanchuma

It is possible that Rabbi Tuchachinsky had in mind the following incredible *Midrash Tanchuma, Parshas Pekudei 3, Gemorah Niddah 16b*, when he prepared his famous parable:

Grieving & Healing

Rabbi Yochanan said, that which it is written (Iyov 9:10) "[G-d] Who performs great deeds that are unfathomable, and limitless wonders." Know that all the souls that were since Adam, the first man, and that will be till the end of the world, all of them were created during the six days of Creation. All of them were in the Garden of Eden; all of them were at the giving of the Torah. As it says (Devorim 29:14) "Those who are standing with us here today and those who are not with us here today." And that which it says "[G-d] Who performs great deeds that are unfathomable" these refer to the great deeds that G-d does when forming the fetus. For when man comes to cohabit with his wife, G-d signals to the angel in charge of conception and says "Know that tonight a person will be formed from the seed of that certain man. Guard the seminal drop, take it, and implant it for storage for 365 parts." The angel then brings the seed before G-d and says to Him: "I have done all that You have commanded me. What will be decreed on this drop?" Immediately, the Almighty decrees what will be the end of this drop - whether male of female, weak or strong, poor or rich, short or tall, ugly or handsome, fat or thin, timid or outgoing. And so He decrees all that will happen to him, all except whether he will be righteous or wicked; that He hands over into the hands of man himself as it says: "See, I have set before you today life and good, death and evil.

Then G-d signals the angel who is in charge of the souls and says to it: "Bring me that certain soul that resides in Gan Eden, whose name is such, and whose appearance is such." for all the souls that are destined to be born were all created from the day the world was created and until the world will end they are all prepared to enter a person...

Immediately the angel goes and brings the soul before G-d. When it appears, it bows and prostrates itself before the King of Kings, the Holy One, blessed is He. At this time G-d commands the spirit to enter that certain seminal drop. The spirit responds: "Master of the Universe, I am satisfied with the world in which I have lived from the day You created me. Why do You wish that I should enter that fetid drop, I who am holy and pure, created from Your glory." At once the Almighty says to the soul: "The world into which I want you to enter will be better for you than the one in which you have lived, and from the time that I formed you. I formed you only with the intent that you should enter this drop."

Immediately G-d forces the soul to enter. After this the angel re-plants the soul in the mother's womb and prepares two angels that will guard it and prevent it form exiting or falling, and kindles a light above his head. This is what it says in Iyov 29:2-3: "Would that I were in my early months, as the days when G-d watched over me. When He lit His candle over my head. etc." And the soul can see from one end of the world t the other.

The angel takes the soul from there and leads it to Gan Eden and shows it the righteous who are sitting in honor, with their crowns upon their heads. The angel says to the soul, "Do you know who these are?" The soul responds, "No, my master." The angel says, "These were formed as

Grieving & Healing

you were in the wombs of their mothers. They went out into the world and kept the Torah and the mitzvos. Therefore they merited all of this good that you see. Know that these merited. But if you do not obey the Torah, you will acquire another place."

That night the angel takes the soul to Gehinnom and shows it the wicked who are being beaten by angels of destruction with fiery sticks. Those souls scream, "Woe, woe," but they receive no pity. Then the angel says to the soul, "Do you know who these are?" And the soul responds,"No, my master." The angel says, "Those being burned were created as you were, exited into the world, but did not keep the Almighty's Torah or His statutes. Therefore they were subjected to the shame that you observes. Know that you, too, will exit into the world. Be righteous, do not be wicked. Then you will merit to live in the World to Come."

Therefore G-d warns him about everything, and the angel accompanies him from morning to night . He shows him the spot where he will die and the place where he will be buried. Then he takes him for a tour of the whole world, showing him the righteous and the wicked-everything.

In the evening he returns him to his mother's womb. G-d makes a barrier, and he dwells in the womb for nine months. During the first three, in the lower chamber; during the next three, in the middle one; and during the last three, in the upper one. When the time comes for him to exit into the air of the world, he rolls and descends in one second from the upper to the middle, and from the middle to the lower. Until that time he eats and drinks from whatever

Grieving & Healing

his mother ate and frank and does not bring forth any excrement.

At the end, his time comes to exit into the world. The angel appears and says to him, "The time has come for you to exit." The soul responds, "Why so you wish to take me out to the world outside?" Says the angel to him, My son, know that you are formed against your will, and now you shall be born against your will. You shall be forced t die and you shall be forced to give a reckoning and account of your actions before the King of Kings, the Holy One, blessed is He."

He does not wish to exit until the angel strikes him, extinguishes the light above his head, and escorts him out into the world by force. Immediately, the baby forgets all that he saw and knew before he exited. Why does that child cry as it exits? Because he has lost his place of rest and respite, the world from which he exited.

At this time, seven worlds and stages of time descend upon him. In the first he is likened to a king; all enquire about his welfare and wish to see him. Everyone wants to hug and kiss him during the first year. In the second year, he is likened to a swine who wallows in the filth. So is the two-year-old who dirties himself with excrements. In the third, he is likened to a goat who jumps from here to there in the good pastures before his mother. So the child gives pleasure to his, mother and father, jumping from here to there, playing, and all delight in him. In the fourth he is likened to a horse that prances in the streets-until he reaches maturity at the age of eighteen. The , just as the

Grieving & Healing

horse runs and takes pride in itself, so, too, the young man prides himself with his youthful strength. In the fifth he is likened to a mule upon which they place a saddle. So, too, with man. They place a burden on him. He marries, bears sons and daughters, goes to and fro in search of his livelihood-until he reaches his fortieth year. In the sixth he is likened to a brazen dog taking from here and there and not feeling any shame. In the seventh (if he reaches senility) he is likened to a monkey, whose countenance is different from all other creatures. He asks constantly for things, eats and drinks like a child ,plays like a baby, and reverts to his youth as far as his mental capacities. Even his children and family members laugh at him. When he speaks, they say to others, "Leave him. He is old, likened to a monkey in all his ways." Even children laugh at him and play with him. Even a free bird will arouse him form his sleep.

When in the end his time comes, the angel comes and says to him, "Do you recognize me?" He responds, "Yes." Then he asks, "Why do you come to me today of all days?" The angel replies, "In order to take you from this world, for the time has come for you to die." Immediately he begins to cry and lets his voce be heard form one end of the world to the other. No creature, however, is able to hear or recognize his voce except for the rooster alone. He then days to the angel, "But you have already taken me out form two worlds and brought me to this world." The angel responds, "Did I not already tell you that you were formed against your will, and your were born against your will"? You were forced to live, you are forced to die, and you are forced to give a

Grieving & Healing

reckoning and accounting of your deeds before the Holy One, blessed is He."

Rabbi Abie Rotenberg's Nishomele

Again, Rabbi Abie Rotenberg has beautifully recorded the message of this Midrash, in his Journeys, II album "*Nishomele:*"

Come with me, little Neshomele, let me hold you in my hand,

And we'll fly away, you and I together, to a place down on the land.

Come with me little Neshomele; don't shy away...do as you're told.

There's a little child waiting to be born today. You're to be his spark, his soul.

But dear Malache'l, no, I don't want to go.

There is so much pain and evil upon the Earth below.

Let me Stay up here in Heaven where it's safe and I'll be pure.

Please don't make me go away. Can't you see I'm so afraid?

Come with me little Noshomele, it's time you faced your destiny.

And as we fly beneath the clouds now I will show you

There is so much you can be.

Yes, dear Malache'l, I can see Kedushah (holiness) over there.

Look, someone's learning Torah; there's another deep in

Grieving & Healing

prayer.

I will stay here if you answer me, it's all I need to know.

You must promise me, dear friend, that I too will be like them.

Come with me, little Neshomele, oh it's a task that I must do.

As I tap you on the lip you will forget me.

You're on your own; it's up to you.

(Music/Passage of Time)

Come with me, little Neshomele, let me hold you in my hand,

And we'll fly away, you and I together, to a place above the land.

But dear Malache'l, no I don't what to go.

I'm not ready to go with you. Where you take me I don't know.

Let me stay right where I am.

There's so much more I need to do.

Please don't make me go away. Can't you see I'm so afraid?

Come with me, little Neshomele, I've only come to take you home.

There is no need to fear your destination.

You've earned a place right by the Throne... A place right by the Throne.

Colonel David (Mickey) Marcus

The essence of Rabbi Tuchachinsky's powerful parable is beautifully stated in the following passage attributed to Colonel David "Mickey" Marcus, as cited in the book "*When Mourning Comes.*" Colonel David (Mickey) Marcus was an American Jew who came to Israel and fought and died in the War of Independence, defending Jerusalem. This passage found on his body:

> "*I am standing upon the seashore. A ship at my side spreads her white sails in the morning breeze and starts for the blue ocean. She is an object of beauty and strength, and I stand and watch her until at length she is only a ribbon of white cloud just where the sea and sky come to mingle with each other. Then someone at my side says, "There! She's gone!" Gone where? Gone from my sight— — that is all. She is just as large in mast and hull and spar as she was when she left my side, and just as able to bear her load of living freight to the place of destination. Her diminished size is in me, not in her, and just at the moment when someone at my side says, "There! She's gone!" there are other voices ready to take up the glad shout "There! She comes!"*

Contemplating and preparing for death, not in an ever-brooding or morbid manner, but in a manner that infuses our lives with a goal and purpose, with a *raison d'etre* for living, changes the very essence of life itself. It keeps us focused on the right path of living, which is to prepare us for life eternal.

January 2010, Comments to a group of Bereaved Parents (non-Jewish)

Mastering the Bounce[5]

We have all experienced a fall from grace. When down and out, we could easily stay there, giving up hope, giving up on our dreams and giving up on themselves, but we didn't. Instead of collapsing, we bounced. And we come back stronger, better and more equipped to achieve greatness than ever before.

That is why I want you to "be the ball." In this metaphor, however, I want you to be the tennis ball. You see, life will smack you around like a tennis ball in a match point between Nadal and Federer.

To win in the game of life you will need to "be the ball" and learn The Bounce.

To bounce: To fall rapidly, hit bottom suddenly with impact and rebound decisively.

According to that definition, there are four distinct phases of The Bounce:

The Fall

We all experience falls in our lives. They don't have to be as traumatic or as devastating as a bankrupcy, divorce, heart attack or life-threatening illness to be considered a fall. Each day we experience minor setbacks and little falls—in discipline

---

5. Inspired by Shai Stern

or poor choices—that require us to bounce back. But there is a difference between falling and failing. The Bounce converts a fall into victory, and the harder you fall, the higher you can bounce.

The Impact

Making impact, hitting bottom, bends you out of shape; your identity—who you thought you were—is morphed and tested. Either you allow the impact to explode you, or you absorb it and use it to spring. Do not lament this phase. While it might be painful in the moment, most often it is the smack of the impact that musters the focus, energy and fight needed to become something you would have never driven yourself to be otherwise. The pain of the impact is what creates the energetic force to launch you in the opposite and positive direction. "You may not realize it when it happens, but a kick in the teeth may be the best thing in the world for you." —Walt Disney

Restoration

The moment when the ball starts to regain its shape… the moment when something inside you starts fighting back against the fall, against the impact. You realize your identity is not defined in the fall; it's defined in your ability to rebound decisively and restore your identity and sense of purpose. You stop mourning where you once were and start focusing on where you are going.

Elevation

You rise again… and most often higher than you were before

Grieving & Healing

The Bounce. Most often it will be because of The Bounce that you are as high as you are today… and as you will reach in the future.

I encourage you to look at your own falls as an opportunity to bounce. Each time you slip and feel the wind of a fall, prepare yourself for impact and get ready to bounce—it might just be exactly what you need to take yourself to new heights.

February 2010, Comments at Hindy's 6th Yahrtzeit Seudah

The Nesivas Sholom on Sarah Imeinu's last minutes & the evil Satan's deadly trick

Tonight I will deal with the *Medrash* that is cited by *Rashi* in *Parchas Chayei Sarah* that says that the Satan told *Sarah Imeinu* that *Avraham Avinu* had slaughtered Yitzchak and that she cried out in grief and died. According to this *Medrash*, the Satan (Angel of Death) was exceedingly perturbed that *Avraham Avinu* was willing to go through with the sacrifice of his son, an act which stands as a merit for his decedents to this day. After repeated attempts at discouraging *Avraham Avinu* failed, the Satan took a different tack. If he couldn't deter Avraham, at least he could scare *Sarah Imeinu* - as they say - to death; literally. He appeared to *Sarah Imeinu* and showed her how in the distance, her beloved and only son Yitzchak lay bound upon the Altar. The hand of her husband Avraham, clenching a sharp knife, stretched towards his neck to perform the ritual slaughter. In the moment just before the sacrifice (Avraham was halted at the very last moment), Sarah was overwhelmed by the vision of her son's slaughter, and in a state of intense shock her soul departed.

It's been suggested that there is no use in bereaved parents trying to heal their broken hearts; as such efforts are futile. They cite this tragic story of Sarah Imeinu's death to prove their point; that bereaved parents cannot possibly be expected to cope with their children's death, and cannot be expected to

Grieving & Healing

'handle it' - the proof being that *Sarah Imeinu* couldn't 'handle it' and died. That if *Sarah Imeinu* couldn't cope with the death of her child Yitzchok, then neither can we.

The purpose of this article is to shed some light on the incident concerning Sarah's death and to show that her death was not a result of *Akeidas Yitzchok*. In the process, important *Hashkafos* of death, dying and bereavement will be revealed shedding new light on the subject.

Parchas Chayei Sarah states that *Sarah Imeinu*'s lifetime was one hundred years, twenty years, and seven years…Sarah died in Kiryas Arba…And Avraham came to eulogize Sarah and to bewail her. (23:1,2,3)

The narrative concerning *Sarah Imeinu*'s passing is indeed enigmatic. First, why does the Torah present the redundancy of the "years"of *Sarah Imeinu*'s life? In fact, the ages of the other *Imahos*, Matriarchs, is not mentioned when the Torah records their deaths. In addition, the *"chaf"* of the word *u'livkosah*, and to bewail her, is written in miniature. The *Baal HaTurim* explains that since *Sarah Imeinu* was very old, the weeping over her passing was diminished. Is this necessary for the *Torah* to note? Additionally, regarding Avraham's eulogizing Sarah, *Rashi* explains the juxtaposition of *Sarah Imeinu*'s death upon the *Akeidas Yitzchak*. He cites *Chazal* who explain that this is done to indicate that she died as a result of that event. The Satan told her that Avraham had actually slaughtered her precious Yitzchak. She cried out in grief and died. We wonder why *Rashi* does not cite this exegesis on the *Pasuk* that records Sarah's death. Rather, he mentions it concerning Avraham's eulogy and mourning for her. Last, Sarah was a woman of

Grieving & Healing

impeccable spiritual ascendancy. How is it that the *Akeidah* catalyzed her death? How could such a *Nisayon*, test, that became the benchmark of Avraham Avinu's distinction, be the ruin of Sarah, who was even greater than he in the area of *Nevius*, prophecy?

The Slonimer Rebbeh, Reb Shalom Noach Brozovski of Slonim, the author of the *Nesivos Shalom* offers a novel interpretation of the proceedings of Sarah's death which elucidates and illuminates the entire narrative.

"V'haseir Satan Milfaneinu U'meiachareinu"

We entreat Hashem daily to *V'haseir Satan Milfaneinu U'meiachareinu*, "Please remove the Satan from before us and from behind us." This indicates that there is a Satan that challenges us in front as we are about to perform a *Mitzvah* or withstand a *Nisoyon*. There is also another Satan, one who attempts to undermine the success and inspiration that we derive upon successfully carrying out a *Mitzvah*. The *Yetzer Hora*, evil-inclination, does everything within its power to sabotage whatever inspiration we might derive from our mitzvah observance. If it does not succeed in preventing us from performing the *Mitzvah*, then it will go to all lengths to frustrate and disenchant us after we have discharged our duty.

The Satan employed every gambit to ensnare Avraham and thwart the successful completion of his mission. When he saw that Avraham had withstood the test, that he had stood there prepared to sanctify Hashem's Name until he was halted by the Angel, he decided to change courses and become the

Grieving & Healing

Satan *Mei'achareinu*, the Satan from behind us. How did he do it? The Satan knew that Sarah was destined to die that day. The Heavenly decree from before her birth was that her lifespan would end on the day that happened to coincide with the *Akeidah*. With this information in his bag of tricks, the Satan told Sarah about what happened to her only son. She immediately died, but not as a result of the shock as the Satan would have everyone believe, but because it was her time. When Avraham heard about the tragedy that had befallen him, and the part that he played in "shortening" Sarah's life, (it appeared that) he regretted the *Akeidah*. That was exactly what the Satan planned. If he could not influence Avraham prior to the *Akeidah*, he would attempt a subterfuge afterwards.

Of course, the Satan failed in his ruse. We now understand why the Torah repeats Sarah's years. This underscores the fact that she lived precisely how long she was destined to live. She did not die "accidentally." Also, we now understand the juxtaposition of Sarah's death upon the *Akeidah*. The Satan wanted everyone to think that she died as a result of Avraham's mission. This is why *Rashi* emphasizes this exegesis on the *Pasuk* that relates that there was decreased mourning for Sarah. She died an old woman. She did not die prematurely. Her time had come, and the mourning was commensurate with this type of loss. It was all "*Maaseh Satan*", the work of the Satan, who was once again foiled in his attempt to impede Avraham Avinu's spiritual progress.

This is why the next *Posuk* in the *Torah* states that "*Vayokom Avrohom MeAl Pnei Meiso*" that Avrohom got up from eulogizing Sarah. While eulogizing Sarah, he entertained a random thought that he was indeed responsible for her death by virtue of his performing the *Akeidah* and he recognized that the isolated thought was a *Maaseh Satan* and he got up and departed from that line of thinking. It wasn't a constructive thought, it didn't advance his *Yiras Shomayim*, and on the contrary, it impeded it. So, "*Vayokom Avrohom*" he severed the thought from his mind and never entertained it again.

There is a very powerful lesson to be derived herein for bereaved parents. We recognize the Satan that confronts us as we are about to withstand a *Nisoyon*. We often ignore him, however, when he comes up from behind. After the painful *Nisoyon* of the death of children, there is a special *Yetzer Hora* that challenges bereaved parents to give up hope and to discourage them from healing. This is the Satan *Mei'achareinu*. This is the "*Maaseh Satan*" who is attempting to impede our spiritual progress.

Grieving & Healing

February 2011, Hindy's 7th Yahrtzeit Seudah

"Samcheinu Keeymos Inisani Shnos Rainu Raah"

A little over thirty years ago, was the bar mitzvah of the son of one of the great rosh hasheshivahs, Rabbi Chaim Mordechai Katz, the former head of the Telshe Yeshivah in Wickliffe, Ohio. He began his speech as follows. The great gaon, Rabbi Aryeh Leib Ginzberg, the Shaagas Aryeh (born 1695, died 1785) held his rabbinic post in the city of Metz. All his life until that time he suffered great poverty. When he first came to Metz he was shown his new home, a beautiful mansion compared to any in which he had lived previously. As he went from room to room admiring the comfortable and spacious living quarters, those around him detected some mumbling of Hebrew words but couldn't hear what the rabbi was saying. When they left the house, one of the more curious baalei batim asked the rabbi what it was he had been saying as he was inspecting the various rooms of the house.

"I'll tell you," said Reb Aryeh. "There is a verse in Psalms (90:15) that says: *"Samcheinu Keeymos Inisani Shnos Rainu Raah"* 'Make us happy [O, God] as the days You have afflicted us; we have seen bad years.' I interpret that to mean that we ask Hashem to give us a cause to rejoice according to the measure of affliction that He metes out to us. When I saw this beautiful mansion I repeated this verse over and over and said to Hashem: Dear Hashem, all my life You have afflicted me with poverty. Now I beseech You, corresponding to that measure of affliction, afford me a corresponding amount of rejoicing and allow me, with Your blessings, to live the rest of my life in comfort and tranquility.

"In the Holocaust I lost a wife and ten children," continued Rabbi Katz. "My prayer to the Ribbono Shel Olom is that He will allow me to rejoice with this son and my other children in corresponding measure to the pain and affliction which He decreed upon me."

I have echoed these sentiments many times. This we are permitted to say to the Almighty: "Dear Hashem, I accept Your decrees, Your affliction, without questioning Your inscrutable ways. I do not murmur against the wisdom of Your secret ways. You are Dayan HaEmes, a true Judge. But please, I beg of You, corresponding to that measure of affliction, bless us with a full measure of joy and happiness with the rest of our loved ones, in health and happiness for length of days."

"Aderabah"

The first paragraph of the Shmoneh Esreh. "*HaKel HaGadol HaGibor Vehanora*" "The great, the mighty, the awesome G-d." The primary importance of the phrase "*HaKel HaGadol HaGibor Vehanora*", as it describes how Hashem directs His power to the world and to us as individuals, and gives structure to the entire berachah. It expresses our confidence in God's omnipotence. But it was not always thus.

YOMA: R' Yehoshua ben Levy said: Why were they called the Anshe Kenesses Hagdolah / the Men of the Great Assembly? Because they returned [Hashem's] glory to its place.

Moshe Rabbeinu, 10:17 in the Plains of Moab, on the verge

Grieving & Healing

of entering the Land, exhorts the Jewish people to do the right thing, he tells them it is because Hashem is the "*HaKel HaGadol HaGibor Vehanora*" Great, Mighty and Awesome God.

Yirmiyahu, 32:18, during the final siege of Jerusalem by Nebuchadnezzar. Jeremiah is in prison, for prophesying the downfall of the Judean kingdom. He has just been given a symbol of the return from exile, buying tribal land from his cousin Hanamel and burying the deed in a jar. He said: "non-Jews are dancing in the courtyard of Your Temple, Gentiles are reveling in His sanctuary, the place of your Awe on Earth; how can I describe You as Awesome?" He emends Moshe's praise to fit the current situation. Where is His awesomeness?" Where is the Norah? and did not say "awesome." And therefore he only said "*HaKel HaGadol HaGibor*" Great & Mighty God. Yirmiyahu, who lived through the destruction of the First Temple and witnessed the terrible devastation and exile, could not see G-d's awesomeness. Certainly he knew that G-d was awesome. But living at that tragic time he could not bring himself to testify about something that seemed to be contradicted by everything he experienced. How could G-d be awesome with all the wanton destruction of His people?

Similarly, Daniel Hanavi lived at a time in which the Jews were humiliatingly subjugated by the Babylonians. Indeed, he was sentenced to be executed for practicing his religion. Daniel then quotes our verse, in the depths of the Babylonian exile. Thinking that the seventy years of Jerusalem's desolation were nearing their end, he prays to God that He send the deliverance soon. As we now know is normal in prayer, he opens with praises of Hashem, "the great and awesome God", but not Mighty. How can he praise God as Mighty, when God is hidden, we are exiled among, and enslaved to, non-Jews? Daniel Hanavi came and said, "Gentiles rule over His sons. Where is His might?"Where the "Gadol?" and he did not say "mighty" And Daniel just said "*HaKel HaGadol Vehanora*" Great, and Awesome God.

Then the Anshei Knesses Hagedolah came, and in constructing the text of the daily prayers, restored Moshe's praise to its full glory. The said and said, *Aderabah,* They reinterpreted Mighty / HaGibor - to describe Hashem's restraint in not fully expressing His anger and destroying the sinful Jews, only demolishing their Temple. This is His might - that he overcomes His desire and is slow to anger [even] over the wicked. They reinterpreted Awesome / HaNorah - Awesome was taken to mean inspiration of the fear of God, without which it would have been impossible for the Jews to continue to exist while exiled among other nations. This is his awesomeness that if not for the fear of G-d how could this one nation survive among the nations?" Thus they wholeheartedly restored the full praise of Moshe into the thrice-daily fundamental prayer.

I too, can relate to Yirmiyahu and Daniel. For I too, had difficulty connecting to certain pieces of the davening after Hindy died. My pain was so intense and so black and so dark, that I thought parts of the Tefilah that were about Simcha, were referring to other people, because Simcha was an alien foreign thought and emotion for me at that time.

I became an editor (sensor) I cut out verses of Simcha - it couldn't possibly apply to me - Yehi Chivod: Ivdu es Hashem

Grieving & Healing

BeSimcha; Nishmas: Ain Anachnu Maspikim Lehodos; Ribbono Shel Olom: Al Kol Hachesed Asher Asah Imi.

The turning point: *Kabbalas Shabbos, Lecha Dodi, Rav Lach Sheves Be'Emek Haboche* - for too long have you dwelled in the Valley of Tears. Hashem became the Healer of the broken heart and the *Rofeh Lishburei Lev* and I began to heal, I began to lessen my grief, and I began to reclaim Simcha. But *Beshaas Maaseh*, while I was in pain ,and in the ditch, I couldn't feel or connect with Simcha. But afterwards, with added perspective, was I able to see God's greatness and his awesomeness. To see how Hashem spared us from far worse calamities and tragedies.

"Vayidom Aharon"

In the aftermath of the tragic deaths of the two sons of Aharon the torah recounts how Moshe approached Aharon apparently in an attempt to comfort him:

> "Then Moshe said to Aharon, Of this did Hashem speak, saying, I will be sanctified through those who are nearest Me, and before the entire People I will be glorified. And Aharon held his peace." *Vayidom Aharon*.

The Torah (Shemos 24:9-11) relates when Moshe and Aharon took Nadav, Avihu, and the seventy elders up to Har Sinai at the time of the giving of the Torah, they "beheld Hash-m, and they ate and drank." Rashi there comments, based on the Midrash, that Nadav and Avihu beheld Hash-m haughtily, when they were satiated with food and drink, and they should have been punished immediately. However, Hash-m did not want to diminish the joy of the giving of the Torah by punishing them at that moment. Instead, He punished them on the day of the inauguration of the Mishkan.

But what if Aharon HaKohein really knew that his sons Nadav, Avihu were destined to die earlier at Har Sinai? What if he knew that Hashem deferred their deaths to give Aharon more time to spend with his children? That no matter the hell of cancer, of chemotherapy and radiation, that that hell was better because we had our daughter, than having her die earlier? Maybe that's why Aharon HaKohein was silent, because he said to himself - thank you Hashem for giving me this extra time with my children, I owe you. Thank you,.

On the 2nd day of Rosh Chodesh Adar II Monday, March 7, 2011, we will commemorate the 7th Yahrtzeit of Hindy. I want to thank Hashem for all that He has done for us. I too, await the great day of Aderabah, where Hashem will show us that all troubles were stepping stones to the Geulah. We will ultimately be reunited with Hindy. *Bilah HaMoves Lanetzach, Umacha Hashem Elokim Dimah Meyal Kol Ponim* - May He swallow up death forever; may Hashem wipe away tears from every face (Isaiah 25:8) *T'hei Nishmasa Tzrurah B'tzror Ha'chaim.*

Grieving & Healing

June 24, 2011, A Message in a Bottle – the Gerrer Rebbe's Letter

I came home thursday night to find three of Hindy's closest friends sitting in our breakfast room chatting with Adina and the kids. They were sitting in the seats they always sat in (erie). My kids looked nervous and happy at the same time, because these girls were great and kept the conversations lively and moving. The empty chair (of Hindy not among us) was killing me. I joined the conversations with my usual upbeat attitude and warmth for them, but inside, I was dying for myself, Adina and the kids. Even though I never "go there" with what couldve been had Hindy lived, that night, seeing Hindy's friends, married and some with kids, forces you to "go there." It was a tough night.

Friday morning in shul, a father beamed with joy as his son returned from Israel to be home for Pesach. The father saw his son, ran up to him to give him a hug and a kiss and said to me: "isn't great to see your child after not seeing him for a while?" THAT killed me and slaughtered me for good. Whatever pain I was carrying in me the night before (that I was hoping would dissipate) was magnified many times over by this innocent exchange.

I not only "went there" but started thinking how wonderful their intact lives are, and how painfully shattered is my splintered destroyed life without my Hindles. It was a horrible Friday morning. I cried my head off during davening and couldn't get through it. Davening helped a bit lightening my burden, but I was still emotionally shell shocked.

Grieving & Healing

I came to my (new) office to see a piece of paper in my fax machine - I received a fax letter.

It was faxed to me by Rabbi Baruch Kupfer that morning (very early - lile at 4:00 am) and it was a letter from the former Gerrer rebbe to a bereaved parent, written 15 years ago. R. Kupfer told me of the letter a month before Hindy's 4th yahrtzeit and said that as soon as he finds it, he'll give me a copy. He found it on Thursday night, and he faxed it to me early Friday morning.

The letter was about reb yochonon's bone (the name of my book). He stated that RY's 10th son by falling into a vat of boiling scalding water. RY took the bone of his 10th son to comfort other bereaved parents. Why?

Now this was precisely THE seminal question that I asked myself when I learned this Gemorah, that led to me naming my book to bereaved parents: *Reb Yochonon's Boe - Chizuk to the Bereaved Parent.*

The Gerrer Rebbe - Reb Pinchos Menachem Alter - wrote (15 years ago) that RY was trying to save the parents from thinking that Hashem is angry with them and is "punishing" them. That since RY was the Godol Hador, he was telling the parents that its happening to him 10x and that it couldn't be that the death of a child is punishment to lead to despair because there was no one greater than RY.

Then the Pnei Menachem (the gerrer rebbe's title) wrote that while he is no RY, he had 2 children die in his lifetime, and wrote of his intense and indescribable pain over the death of his son Yehuda, and how he was seized by the notion that Hashem's pain over it was far greater than our pain, and how

Grieving & Healing

this epiphany lightened the bitterness of his grief somewhat.

Finally, the letter concluded with a novel Chiddush: that friends have a Halachic obligation to attempt to comfort and console the bereaved parent, yet, at the same time, the bereaved parent has a mitzvah to accept the consolations being offered.

The letter ends with a heartfelt prayer for Techias Hameisim and Moshiach, when we will be reunited with our children.

I sat in my office weeping uncontrollably, at the timing and at the message in the bottle, and at this time capsule, that Hashem sent to me in one of my darkest hours to heal my broken heart over hindy's death and absence before Pesach.

I felt that I now had a Kesher to the Gerrer Rebbe.

I could go on about the magnificence and elegance of the letter. It occurred to me how healing reading it was, and how healing my book is to others who have read it. It's a shame that for now, its only for family and the closest of the close.

That's it. I received a message in the bottle from the Gerrer Rebbe. I'm entering Pesach with less tears and with purity.

Grieving & Healing

November 11, 2011 – Comments to a group of Bereaved Parents, quoting from The Jigsaw Puzzle; Kitchen Table Wisdom by Dr. Rachel Naomi Remen[6]

All through my childhood, my parents kept a giant jigsaw puzzle set up on a puzzle table in the living room. My father, who had started all this, always hid the box top. The idea was to put the pieces together without knowing the picture ahead of time. Different members of the family and visiting friends would work on it, sometimes for only a few minutes at a time, until after several weeks hundreds and hundreds of pieces would each find their place.

Over the years, we finished dozens of these puzzles. In the end I got quite good at it and took a certain satisfaction in being the first one to see where a piece went or how two grounds of pieces fit together. I especially loved the time when the first hint of pattern would emerge and I could see what had been there, hidden, all along.

The puzzle table was my father's birthday present to my mother. I can see him setting it up and gleefully pouring the pieces of that first puzzle from the box onto the table top. I was three or four and I did not understand my mother's delight. They hadn't explained this game to me, doubtless thinking I was too young to participate. But I wanted to participate, even then.

Alone in the living room early one morning, I climbed on a chair and spread out the hundreds of loose pieces lying on

---

6. Inspired by Rabbi Aron Dov Friedman

Grieving & Healing

the table. The pieces were fairly small; some were brightly colored and some dark and shadowy. The dark ones seemed like spiders or bugs, ugly and a little frightening. They made me feel uncomfortable. Gathering up a few of these, I climbed down and hid them under one of the sofa cushions. For several weeks, whenever I was alone in the living room, I would climb up on the chair, take a few more dark pieces, and add them to the cache under the cushion.

So this first puzzle took the family a very long time to finish. Frustrated, my mother finally counted the pieces and realized that more than a hundred were missing. She asked me if I had seen them. I told her then what I had done with the pieces I didn't like and she rescued them and completed the puzzle. I remember watching her do this. As piece after dark piece was put in place and the picture emerged, I was astounded. I had not known there would be a picture. It was quite beautiful, a peaceful scene of a deserted beach. Without the pieces I had hidden, the game had made no sense.

Perhaps winning requires that we love the game unconditionally. Life provides all the pieces. When I accepted certain parts of life and denied and ignored the rest, I could only see my life a piece at a time - the happiness of a success or a time of celebration, or the ugliness and pain of a loss or a failure I was trying hard to put behind me out of sight. But like the dark pieces of the puzzle, these sadder events, painful as they are, have proven themselves a part of something larger. What brief glimpses I have had of something hidden seem to require accepting as a gift every last piece.

We are always putting the pieces together without knowing the picture ahead of time. I have been with many people in times of profound loss and grief when an unsuspected meaning begins to emerge from the fragments of their lives. Over time, this meaning has proven itself to be durable and trustworthy, even transformative. It is a kind of strength that never comes to those who deny their pain.

Grieving & Healing

February 2012, Hindy's 8th Yahrtzeit Seudah

It's Happening Again[7]

It's happening again. And it seems that there is nothing that I can do to stop it. Each breath comes with more difficulty, my eyes grow heavy with tears, my chest constricts as if it is being both crushed by a weight and struggling against being torn apart from within. My limbs are as heavy as if I had the flu. I want to shut out the world and ignore it—but I know that it just won't go away. It's that time of the year—the anniversary of my daughter Hindy's death is coming this 2nd day of Rosh Chodesh Adar and tonight will be the first in a series of memorial events in her honor.

Even though its been eight years already—even though the image of my daughter's death and levayah are etched forever in my memory—I still catch myself wondering if it ever really happened. Was it me sitting at her bed, at her funeral, standing at her grave saying Kaddish? Could it really be that my beautiful Hindy has gone? Like the implausibility of winning the lottery, the chance that it was my daughter to be stricken and die from cancer still seems too remote to be real. But I know that it was all too so.

Each year since then, and each and every time I find myself drawn back to that horrible day of February 23, 2004 at 4:33pm, my heart breaks anew. I can actually feel it tear in two, like the suit jacket that I wore to her funeral which was slit and

---

7. Inspired by Naftoli Moses, the father of Avrohom Dovid Moses, brutally killed at the Mercaz HaRav massacre.

torn over my chest. My eyes well up with tears and my voice catches. I want to scream, but can't, the pain is so deep. Yet, yet I can't let go of these memories, and I won't.

Elie Wiesel, one of our people's most profound exponents of tragic memory (speaking against the backdrop of Ronald Reagan's troubling presidential visit to the final resting place of dozens of Nazi Waffen-SS troops in Bitburg, Germany) stated that *"if there is one word that defines the fragility, the vulnerability but also the invincibility of the human condition, it is memory."* To forget, to allow all that is left of my beloved daughter to vanish into the vaporous wisps of time seems to be as unimaginable as was her loss. How can I? With this, I begin....

"Baruch Gozer U'mekayeim"

Horav Eliezer Zisha Portugal, zl, the Skulener Rebbe, did everything within his power to bring Jews closer to their faith. In fact, he would convince young men not to join the Romanian army lest they become lost to Yiddishkeit in the harmful environment. Instead, he encouraged them to go to a yeshivah where they would study Torah and strengthen their faith. As it would be, someone reported the Rebbe's "seditious" activities to the authorities, who promptly arrested him. He was thrown into a horribly disgusting dirty cell, bereft of any amenities for maintaining cleanliness or hygiene. His Yarmulkeh and glasses were taken from him. The Rebbe was a frail, sickly man, who would not be able to survive very long in this cold, dirty dungeon.

Grieving & Healing

What could he do to maintain his sanity under such horrible conditions? He began to daven. The Rebbe's kavanah, concentration, during tefillah was legendary. He prayed for hours with incredible devotion, entreating the Almighty on behalf of His people. In this extraordinary predicament one can imagine that he poured out his heart with even greater fervor and emotion. He enunciated every word with the greatest passion, the entire tefillah constituted a lesson in *Avodas Hashem*.

The Rebbe was troubled by something that grabbed his gut, in the prayer of *"Baruch She'omar"*. This *Tefilah* praises Hashem for all the wonderful, positive things he was doing for us. *Baruch SheAmar VeHaya HaOlom* Blessed is He Who spoke and the world came into being; *Baruch Omor VeAshe* Blessed is He Who speaks and does; *Baruch Merachemn Al Haaretz* - Blessed is He who has compassion on the earth; Baruch Meshalem Sachar Tov LiReAyhu - Blessed is He who rewards to those who fear Him; *Baruch Chai LawOd VeKayem Lanetzach* - Blessed is He who lives forever and endures to eternity; *Baruch Podeh Umatzil* - Blessed is He who redeems and rescues; and then he got to the clause *Baruch Gozer UmeKayem* - Blessed is He who decrees and fulfills - and he froze.

He, like all of us, had recited this prayer countless times over the years. Suddenly, he was bothered by the word "*Gozer U'mekayeim*", "He decrees and fulfills." This phrase did not belong in the tefillah. It did not fit in. The phrase, "*gozer u'mekayeim*", seems out of place. A gezeirah, decree, is usually an edict that carries with it very harsh ramifications; a negative

Grieving & Healing

phenomenon, a seemingly evil decree. Why then are we thanking Hashem for carrying out this evil decree?

The Skelener Rebbe pondered this phrase for days and days, attempting to ascertain exactly what this prayer was referring to. "Baruch *gozer u'mekayeim*, Baruch *gozer u'mekayeim*, Baruch *gozer u'mekayeim*," He decrees and fulfills. The Rebbe announced to himself, "I will not leave this prison cell, even if I am freed, until I uncover the meaning behind this phrase."

Finally, insight came; revelation dawned upon him. The word "*U'mekayeim*" "fulfills" does not refer to the Al-mighty who issues the decrees -- the subject of the verse. Rather, it refers to mankind, the object. Hashem enacts the decree and also gives (or has given) us the strength to endure it, to withstand the trial. In understanding this verse, we must read it, "Blessed is He who decrees and enables us to fulfill, to endure and to perservere."

There are times when, for reasons beyond our understanding, Hashem must issue a harsh and painful decree against an individual. This decree can have a devastating effect upon the person. How can he "make it" through all the suffering that was assigned to him. The answer is, "*Baruch Gozer U'mekayeim*". While it is true that Hashem makes the gezeirah, He is also "me'kayeim", He gives succor and strength to the person to persevere. Hashem sustains the individual, giving him the fortitude to endure the crisis that has challenged him. The Skulener Rebbe realized that while he was the victim of a serious decree, Hashem would sustain him and enable him to prevail over his torment. His attitude changed and he was released from his predicament a few days later. Every year on

Grieving & Healing

the anniversary of his release from prison, the Rebbe would recount this episode in his life and explain to those assembled how Hashem sustains those who are true objects of his *Gezeirah*.

This powerful story resonates very deeply within me, on the 8th Yahrtzeit of our daughter Hindy. The tragedy of her illness and death was indeed the darkest chapter of our lives. Yet the lesson of the *Baruch She-Amar*, is that we are not to be broken by events that challenge us, as painful as they are, because Hashem gives us the strength to overcome. Hashem gives us the ability to overcome the painful challenge, to triumph over the pain, to accept the tragic loss with courage and faith and to go on. In truth, it is only with such Divine assistance that one can "make it." Hence the genius of *Baruch Gozer U'mekayeim*

Yaakov's Avinu's Silence

In *Parshas VaYishlach*, the love of Yaakov Avinu's life, Rochel Imeinu dies tragically while giving birth to Binyomin, and there is no description whatsoever, of Yaakov Avniu's pain or his tears. A great silence envelops this episode. As a matter of fact, looking at Yaakov's role during her death, all we know is that as she was dying, he took the time to change the name that she herself had given to her newborn son. She called him Ben Oni - son of my grief, and he named him Binyomin - son of my strength.

The situation is different in the case of Avraham Avinu, whose reaction to the death of his wife, Sarah, in her old age merits a detailed description at the beginning of *Parshas Chayei Sarah*.

Grieving & Healing

Unlike Sarah's death, regarding Rachel, there is no mention of her husband coming to eulogize her and to mourn for her.

Of the three Avos, Yaakov Avinu is the one who gives the greatest verbal expression to his emotions. In fact, Yaakov Avinu cried when he first met Rochel: *"Vayishok Ya'akov le'Rachel, Vayisa es kolo Vayeivk"* "Yaakov kissed Rachel, and he raised his voice and cried." (Bereishis 29:11) Rashi explains that Yaakov cried because he foresaw that Rachel would not be buried with him. (ie., that she would die on the road to Ephrath, which is Bethlehem, not be buried in the *MeAras Hamachpelah*.

We don't even have a *VaYidom Aharon* - that Yaakov was silent in response to Rochel's death. We have nothing. No reaction from Yaakov.

Against this background, Yaakov's silence in our story, and the silence of the narrative itself, is all the more stark. We hear neither a broken-hearted cry nor any description of an act of mourning. What is the meaning of this silence?

Yaakov's Harsh Response to Rochel's Plea for Children[8]

To understand this, we need to go back in time to the last recorded conversation between Yaakov & Rochel: Recall that Rachel was barren and unable to conceive children. She asked Yaakov to pray to Hashem for her to have children, and Yaakov Avinu's response to her was quite harsh. In order to understand why Yaakov Avinu was quiet during Rachel's death, we need

---

8. Inspired by the Kosover Rebbe of Boro Park, HaRav Shraga Feivish Hager.

Grieving & Healing

to understand why Yaakov Avinu was harsh with Rachel when she requested children:

Rochel Imeinu's Great Merit

We know that it is the human nature (*Tevah*) of a person, that when they do something extraordinary for Hashem, they expect something extraordinary back from Hashem. Rachel Imeinu, did something extraordinary for Hashem, In order to understand what she did that was so extraordinary, let us look at the *Medresh Eicha* for the background:

At the time of the destruction of the first *Bais Hamikdash*, the Medresh details Hashem's conversations with Yirmiyahu Hanavi, Avraham, Yitzchak, Yaakov, Moshe .... and Rachel. The setting for those conversations was their attempts at changing Hashem's decision to keep the Jews in exile after having destroyed the *Bais Hamikdash*. Yirmiyahu HaNavi at the time of the Churban was told to summon the Avos and Moshe so that their tears might move Hashem to be forgiving. Yirmiyahu did as he was told and Avraham, Yitzchak, Yaakov, and Moshe presented their arguments on behalf of their wayward children.

Avraham argued that mercy was due because of the merits of his readiness to bring Yitzchak as a Korban at the Akeidah. Yitzchak argued that mercy was due because of the merits of his willingness to submit to the Akeidah. Yaakov argued that mercy was due because of the merits of his lifetime of trial and tribulation in protecting and raising his children to become the Jewish nation. Moshe argued that mercy was due because of the merits of his tireless commitment and devotion

Grieving & Healing

to the Jewish people in shepherding them through 40 years of challenge and rebellion. Their common theme was, "There are personal merits on record that You (Hashem) are not taking into account in making Your decision. If You would take those merits into account You would be merciful, and bring the Jews home. In each instance, Hashem listened to their pleas but did not respond. Hashem did not counter their arguments, nor did He offer any explanations. He simply did not respond.

In the middle of Moshe's presentation the Medresh records that Rachel interrupted Moshe to make her plea. Let us pick up the conversation at that point - to see what she did that was so extraordinary.

> *"Master of the Universe, You know that Your servant Yaakov truly loved me, and worked seven years for my father, in order to marry me. At the conclusion of those seven years, when it was time for me to marry my husband, my father wanted to switch my sister for me allowing Leah to marry Yaakov. I found out my father's intentions and was very pained and bothered. I shared my father's intentions with Yaakov and gave him secret signs (Simanim) so that he would know if the person he was to marry was me or someone else. Later, I regretted giving Yaakov the secret signs. I decided to overcome my personal desires and hopes for marrying Yaakov and have mercy on my sister. I gave her the secret signs so that she would not be shamed when it was discovered, that she was Leah and not me. More so than that, I secreted myself beneath the conjugal bed that night so that I could answer any question Yaakov may have posed during the night ensuring that the differences*

Grieving & Healing

in our voices would not give Leah away. In the end, I was merciful and kind to my sister, and I was not jealous of her. Master of the Universe, if I, a mere mortal of flesh and blood, was not jealous of my sister and did not allow her to be shamed and embarrassed, how much more so should it be with You! As the Almighty and Eternal Master of the Universe You should not be jealous of idols just as I was not jealous of Leah! Why did You allow the Bais Hamikdash to be destroyed, my children to be exiled, and the enemy to do with them whatever they wished! Why would You do such a thing?"

Immediately, G-d's mercy was aroused and He said to Rachel (we recite this prophecy as the Haftorah of the second day of Rosh HaShana); 'Because of you I will return the Jews to their rightful place.' *Ve'shavu Banim Li'gvulam.*

As the verses in Yirmiyah 31:14-15 state: *Kol Beramah Nishma* ... "So did G-d proclaim, 'A voice on high was heard; *Rachel Mevakah Al Baneha* Rachel cries for her children - and refuses to be consoled; *Min'i Kolech Mibechi Ve'enecha Midimah* Therefore G-d said, stop your cries and dry your tears; *Ve'shavu Banim Li'gvulam* your children will return to their boundaries."

So the payment to Rochel Imeinu for her out-of-ordinary sacrifice will be that at the end of days, and at the end of time, when Klal Yisroel is facing the threat of annihilation: the payback will be that Hashem will end our bitter Golus, bring Moshiach, and bring His children home - to payback the debt to Rochel.

Payback

And now we come full circle: When Rochel asked Yaakov

for children, Yaakov knew about all this, he knew about the prophechies of Yirmiyahu Hanavi, he knew the *Keitz* - the end of days, and appealed to Rochel, that if Hashem were to pay her back with a child through his efforts, her debt would have ben paid, and what will be Klal Yisroel's merit be when we face destruction? What merit will we have to bring Moshiach? If we use up merits to get you a child now, your debt would be paid. So as tragic as your situation is, Rochel, it has to be this way, in order so that Hashem will bring us home, *Ve'shavu Banim Li'gvulam*. And that's why Yaakov Avinu was quiet when Rochel died. Because it had to happen that way.

This too, is of great meaning to me on Hindy's Yahrtzeit. There is some comfort and consolation in knowing that it had to happen this way. That Hindy's lease on life was destined and only meant to be 17.5 years, and that the last 2.5 of them were to be very challenging. That Hashem's ways are just and perfect. That Hashem has a master plan, and that one day, *Ve'shavu Banim Li'gvulam* He will bring home the children of this shul who have been taken away early: Hindy Cohen, Shaya Twersky and Moishie Rubin

On the 2nd day of Rosh Chodesh Adar I Friday February 24, 2012, we will commemorate the 8th Yahrtzeit of Hindy. I want to thank Hashem for all that He has done for us. I too, await the great day where we will ultimately be reunited with Hindy. *Bilah HaMoves Lanetzach, Umacha Hashem Elokim Dimah Meyal Kol Ponim* - May He swallow up death forever; may Hashem wipe away tears from every face (Isaiah 25:8) *T'hei Nishmasa Tzrurah B'tzror Ha'chaim.*

February 2013, Hindy's 9th Yahrtzeit Seudah

On the 2nd day of *Rosh Chodesh Adar*, Monday, February 11, 2013 we will commemorate the 9th *Yahrtzeit* of our daughter Hindy. ... 9 years .....

Ki Azi "Vezimros" Kah[9]

Every *Motzoi Shabbos* we welcome in the new week, with the words of *Havdallah*: "*Hinei Kel Yeshuasee Eftach Velo Efchad Ki Azi Vezimros Kah*" - Behold! *Hashem* is my salvation. I shall trust and not fear, for *Hashem* is my might and my praise/song. *Ki Azi "Vezimros" Kah* (Yeshayah 12:2).

The Hebrew word "*Zimrah*" has various meanings. It can mean song, from the word "*Zemer;*" it can also mean the most praiseworthy, as in Yaakov Avinu's instruction to his sons "*Kechu Mizimras Haaretz*" take from that which is most praiseworthy (Bereishis 43:11); and it can also mean to prune as the Gemorah in Shabbos (73b) says: "*Zomer Chayav Mishum Note'a*" (pruning is *Chayav* because of planting). When one has a tree with an inferior branch that is drawing nourishment from the mother tree, thereby taking away nutrition from the good branches, the bad branch is pruned, cut away, for the sake of the others.

Tonight on the eve of my daughter 9th Yahrtzeit, all aspects of the word *Zimrah* are applicable. "*Kechu Mizimras Haaretz*" take from the best; that would be my daughter Hindy. She really was a great kid. She was from the best. Perhaps she

---

9. Inspired by Rabbi Paysach Krohn

was ... 'plucked' from us at a young age or "pruned" from our tree, so that she would be an atonement for others, and that is perhaps why were are able to sing about her life 9 years later, because in the depth of our souls we understand that she *may* have saved us.

Ben Oni vs Benyamin

The most emotionally wrenching episode in *Parshas Vayishlach* is the death of Rachel Imeinu during the birth of Binyamin. Recall, that on the way to *Eretz Yisroel*, Rachel Imeinu went into childbirth, and the midwife indicated that it was a son. Rachel Imeinu's labor was extremely difficult, and ultimately proved fatal. The *Pasuk* (35:18) records that in her last dying breath, Rachel Imeinu named her son "*Ben Oni*," but that "his father" (i.e., Yaakov Avniu) called him "*Binyamin*."

As Rachel Imeinu breathed her last breath on this world, knowing fully well that she was about to die, she named her son "Ben Oni" meaning the son of my pain. Obviously she went through great pain in order to bring him into the world. Yet Yaakov Avinu ignored her dying wish and called him "Binyomin" instead - son of my strength.

Why would Rachel Imeinu give such a depressing name to her son "Ben Oni" and how could Yaakov Avinu change it?

I gave a lot of thought to this brief exchange between Binyomin's parents over his name that is wedged into the *Posuk* of Rochel Imeinu's death, I reflected heavily on what exactly was Rachel's pain, what was her dying message to her son, and what was Yaakov's response, and who was right? I

Grieving & Healing

have concluded that this enigmatic *Posuk* contains powerful insights into pain, powerful lessons on how to grieve properly, and finally inspiring lessons on how to go forward in life after a tragedy.

But first, let us try to imagine the scene leading to the birth of this child as it unfolded, and the conversation that I suspect *might* have transpired between Yaacov Avinu and Rachel Imeinu. After being childless for so many years, Rachel Imeinu is finally blessed with her second son. After yearning and praying for decades, her prayers are at last answered. She is lying in bed. She is dying--and she knows it! She is about to be separated forever from the only man she ever loved--and she knows it! She will never reside in Eretz Yisroel--and she knows it! She will never be able to raise this 2nd child of hers--and she knows it! And she is consumed by pain! She looks at her newborn son, and while searching for the appropriate name for him, she is so overcome with pain and grief, that she chooses a name that embodies her emotions: "*Ben Oni*" - the child of my suffering.

In my research into this Posuk, I discovered two incredible insights that shed light into the private world of turmoil that Rachel Imeinu carried within her:

First, the *Chasam Sofer*: The reason Rachel Imeinu died when they came into Eretz Yisroel is that Yaakov Avinu and all the *Avos* kept all the *Mitzvos* while in *Eretz Yisroel*. Since he couldn't be married to two sisters, Rachel Imeinu being the second sister he married was doomed to death upon their return from *Chutz La'Aretz* into *Eretz Yisroel*. This all happened to Rachel Imeinu because of the strength and courage that she showed

Grieving & Healing

in helping her sister Leah marry Yaakov on what was to be her wedding night. Rachel Imeinu's death was yet another painful chapter and yet another tragic consequence of her heroic and selfless act. And hence, her intense pain culminating at that moment.

Second, from Rav Yaakov Meidan, the Rosh Yeshiva Har Etzion: In *Parshas Vayeitze*, Rachel Imeinu steals her father's *Terafim* (idols) (Bereishis 31:19) and she now believes that her death is a consequence of her sin. Hence, she names her son "Ben Oni" (literally, "the son of my sin"). In contrast, Yaakov Avinu understands his wife's death to be a result of *his* vow to Lavan that the one who took the *Terafim* will surely die. Therefore, he calls his son Binyamin (literally, "the son of the right [hand]" in the Torah, oaths are frequently represented by the right hand). In other words, instead of accusing each other and blaming each other, both Yaakov Avinu and Rachel Imeinu assumed responsibility and shouldered the blame for Rachel Imeinu's death. Again, this was her internal pain.

But that addresses the agonizing pain as to why Rachel Imeinu named her son Ben Oni. This still begs the question even more! How could Yaakov Avinu deny his dying wife's wish? This seems rather strange. What's wrong with the name "Ben Oni?" If this was Rachel's last wish, shouldn't he have kept the name she so greatly desired? Why change it?

The Ramban points out that the word *"Oni"* really has two meanings. It *can indeed* mean strength as in *"Raiyshis Oni,"* or it can mean very deep sorrow and pain. On the day of someone's death, a close relative who must mourn for him is *Halachically* called an *"Onein."* The day of death is the most

Grieving & Healing

painful day in a person's life. Perhaps Rachel Imeinu called her son "Ben Oni" so that he would always remember the great pain she was willing to suffer in order to bring a son into this world. In fact, on the very day of his birth Binyomin was actually considered an *Onein*. By naming him "Ben Oni" he would always remember how much he meant to her. That she was willing to sacrifice her own life for him. He was to remember this lesson every day of his life. In fact he would be celebrating his birthday on the very day of her *Yahrtzeit*, on the day he had once been an *Onein*. Her subtle message to him may have been that he should always prove himself worthy so that she wouldn't have suffered in vain. Every day of his life he'd be reminded that his mother had given up her own life so that he could come into this world and would try to live up to her great expectations. Hence the name "Ben Oni."

According to the Ramban, Yaakov Avinu may well have been worried that Binyomin may subconsciously blame himself, for his mother's death. After all, if not for him, she would still have lived. While it certainly wasn't his fault; it was his birth that was responsible for his mother's death. This very thought could haunt a very sensitive person for the rest of his life. To be reminded of this fact on a daily basis may be too much for him to bear. Every time someone would call him by his name "Ben Oni" it would somehow remind him of that tragedy that occurred on the day of his birth, and that his mother suffered and had died on his account. Yaakov Avinu probably felt that this was far too much for a person to bear, and so he decided to change his son's name. Yet he didn't change it completely. He kept the first part of the name "Ben" and only changed the second part.

The Ramban suggests that Yaakov Avinu both wanted to honor Rachel Imeinu and sweeten her bitter words at the same time. The Ramban says that he changed the word "Oni" which can also mean strength to the word "Yemin" which also connotes strength or power, since it is the right hand which is the strong and powerful one. In other words, Yaakov Avinu respected and honored Rachel Imeinu's choice of names, but disagreed with her about its meaning.

I understand this amazing Ramban as follows: At that agonizing moment, Rachel saw pessimism and finality, that her family would celebrate Binyamin's birth while they were sitting *Shiva* for her, that she would never know him, and he would never know her, making little orphan Binyamin into a tragic case. Nor was she wrong!

But at that same gut-wrenching moment, Yaakov Avinu instead saw optimism and possibility, strength and hope, in Binyamin. He refused to dwell on the past and only looked to Binyamin's future.

Binyomin's birth was rooted in the tragedy of his mother's death, but also symbolizes a triumph of completion. The *Shiftei-Kah* - the twelve tribes became complete when Binyamin was born, the journey of Yaakov was completed. In the end, even the *Bais Hamikdosh* was to be built in the territory of Binyamin partly because of what Binyamin's birth represented.

Yaakov lived perhaps the hardest and most punishing life of all the *Avos*. Yet, when he looked down at his new baby boy - Binyamin - rather than succumbing to the tragedy and the

Grieving & Healing

realization of what he had lost, he instead focused on that which he had gained, a special son, a *Ben Zekunim*, a child of his old age, a memorial to Rachel Imeinu.

Yaakov Avinu was a relentless optimist. In each challenge that came his way, he found reason for hope and inspiration. When the rock covered the well, he did not dwell on how impossible it would be to move it, he just did what he had to do. When he was fooled into marrying Leah, he did not write sad poetry about it; he went back to work for Rachel Imeinu. When Lavan tried to cheat him, he did not play the victim, he just figured out a way to turn the tables. And when Rachel Imeinu died - tragically and suddenly - he found joy in his son and kept moving forward.

May we be like Yaakov Avinu, recognizing the good that we have and being irrepressibly optimistic about the future. *Bilah HaMoves Lanetzach, Umacha Hashem Elokim Dimah Meyal Kol Ponim* - May He swallow up death forever; may Hashem wipe away tears from every face (Isaiah 25:8) *T'hei Nishmasa Tzrurah B'tzror Ha'chaim.*

July 28, 2013, Comments at Oscherowitz Sheva Berachos

Broken: Why Breaking the Tablets Was Moshe Rabbeinu' Greatest Accomplishment[10]

"The world breaks everyone, and afterwards some are stronger in the broken places." -- Ernest Hemingway

Broken

The simple reading of the story (recorded in the week's Torah portion, Eikev - the Shabbos of Dani's Aufruf) goes like this: After Klal Yisroel created an Eigal HaZahav, the Golden Calf, Moshe Rabbeinu smashed the stone tablets created by Hashem, engraved with the Aseres Hadibros, the Ten Commandments. Moshe Rabbeinu and Hashem then "debated" the appropriate response to this transgression and it was decided that if the people would truly repent, Hashem would give them a second chance. Moshe Rabbeinu hewed a second set of stone tablets; Hashem engraved them also with the Aseres HaDibros, and Moshe Rabbeinu gave them to Klal Yisroel.

Yet a few major questions come to mind.

Moshe Rabbeinu, outraged by the sight of a Eigal HaZahav erected by Klal Yisroel as a deity, smashed the stone tablets. He apparently felt that Klal Yisroel was undeserving of them, and that it would be inappropriate to give them this Divine gift. But why did Moshe Rabbeinu have to break and shatter the

---

10. Inspired by Rabbi YY Jacobson

Grieving & Healing

heavenly tablets? Moshe Rabbeinu could have hidden them or returned them to their heavenly maker?

The Chachamim teach us that "The whole tablets and the broken tablets nestled inside the Aron, the Ark of the Covenant. (Talmud Bava Basra 14a)" Klal Yisroel proceeded to gather the broken fragments of the first set of tablets and had them stored in the Aron, in the Mishkan, together with the second whole tablets. Both sets of tablets were later taken into Eretz Yisroel and kept side by side in the Aron, situated in the Kodesh HaKadashim in the Bais Hamikdosh in Yerushalayim.

This seems strange. Why would they place the broken tablets in the Kodesh Kodoshim? After all, these fragments were a constant reminder of the great moral failure of Klal Yisroel. (On Yom Kippur, the holiest day of the year, the Kohein Godol would not perform the service with his usual golden garments, since gold was remotely reminiscent of the golden calf. Yet in this instance, throughout the entire year, the very symptom of the golden calf – the broken tablets – were stored in the Kodosh Kodoshim! Cf. Ramban and Ritva to Bava Basra ibid; Likkutei Sichos vol 26 Parshas Ki Sisa.) Why not just disregard them, or deposit them in a safe isolated place?

In its eulogy for Moshe Rabbeinu, the Torah chooses this episode of smashing the Luchos as the highlight and climax of Moshe Rabbeinu' achievements.

In the closing verses of Devorim - Parshas VeZos HaBracha we read: "Moshe, the servant of Hashem, died there in the land of Moab... And there arose not since a prophet in Israel like Moshe, whom Hashem knew face to face; all the signs

Grieving & Healing

and wonders which G-d sent to do in the land of Egypt... that mighty hand, those great fearsome deeds, which Moshe did before the eyes of all Israel."

What did Moshe Rabbeinu do "before the eyes of all Israel?" Rashi, in his commentary on Torah, explains "That his heart emboldened him to break the Luchos before their eyes, as it is written, 'and I broke them before your eyes.' Hashem's opinion then concurred with his opinion, as it is written, 'which you broke—I affirm your strength for having broken them.'" Yasher Koach.

This is shocking. Following all of the grand achievements of Moshe Rabbeinu, the Torah chooses to conclude its tribute to Moshe Rabbeinu by alluding to this episode of breaking the Luchos! Granted that Moshe Rabbeinu was justified in breaking the Luchos, but can this be said to embody his greatest achievement? How about his taking Klal Yisroel out of Egypt? Molding them into a people? Splitting the Yam Suf? Receiving the Torah from Hashem and transmitting it to humanity? Shepherding them for forty years in a wilderness?

Why does the Torah choose this tragic and devastating episode to capture the zenith of Moshe Rabbeinu' life and as the theme with which to conclude the entire Torah, all Chamisha Chumshei Torah!

In the Fragments

We need to examine this entire episode from a deeper vantage point.

Moshe Rabbeinu did not break the Luchos because he was

Grieving & Healing

angry. Rather, the breaking of the Luchos was the beginning of the healing process. Before the Eigal HaZahav was created, Klal Yisroel could find Hashem within the wholesomeness of the tablets, within the spiritual wholesomeness of life. Now, after the people have created the Eigal HaZahav, hope was not lost. Now they would find Hashem in the shattered pieces of a once beautiful dream.

Moshe Rabbeinu was teaching the Jewish people the greatest message of Judaism: Truth could be crafted not only from the spiritually perfected life, but also from the broken pieces of the human corrupt and demoralized psyche. The broken tablets, too, possess the secret of Hashem.

Which is why the Chachamim tell us that not only the whole tablets, but also the broken ones, were situated in the holy of holies. This conveyed the message articulated at the very genesis of Judaism: From the broken pieces of life you can create a holy of holies.

Hashem, the sages tell us, affirmed Moshe Rabbeinu' decision to break the tablets. Hashem told him, "Thank you for breaking them. (See Talmud Shabbas 87a and rashi ibid; Rashi to Deut. 34:12, the final verse of the Torah.)" Because the broken Luchos, representing the shattered pieces of human existence, have their own story to tell; they contain a light all their own. Truth is found not only in wholesomeness, but also—sometimes primarily—in the broken fragments of the human spirit (G-d said to Moses: 'Do not be distressed over the First Tablets, which contained only the Ten Commandments. In the Second Tablets I am giving you, you will also have Halachah, Midrash and Aggadah" (Midrash Rabbah, Shemot 46:1.) This means, that it was precisely the breaking of the tablets that became the catalyst for a far deeper divine revelation). There are moments when Hashem desires that we connect to Him as wholesome people, with clarity and a sense of fullness; there are yet deeper moments when He desires that we find Him in the shattered experiences of our lives.

We hope and pray to always enjoy the "whole tablets," but when we encounter the broken ones, we ought not to run from them or become dejected by them; with tenderness we ought to embrace them and bring them into our "holy of holies," recalling the observation of the Kotzker Rebbe, "there is nothing more whole than a broken heart."

We often believe that Hashem can be found in our moments of spiritual wholesomeness. But how about in the conflicts which torment our psyches? How about in the very conflict we experience between a godless existence and a Hashem-centered existence? We associate "religion" with "religious" moments. But how about our "non-religious" moments?

What Moshe Rabbeinu accomplished with breaking the Luchos was the demonstration of the truth that the stuff we call Kedusha and holiness can be carved out from the very alienation of a person from Hashem. From the very turmoil of his or her psychological and spiritual brokenness, a new holiness can be discovered.

It is on this note that the Torah chooses to culminate its tribute to Moshe Rabbeinu' life. The greatest achievement of Moshe Rabbeinu was his ability to show humanity how we can take our brokenness and turn it into a Kodesh Kodoshim.

September 13, 2013: Comments at Orthodox Jewish Bereaved Parents Support Group

Lesson of Survival Derived from an innocent Rashi in Parshas Pinchos

The Torah states (Bereishis 12:15) that: "When Pharaoh's officials saw her (Sarah), they praised her for Pharaoh, and the woman was taken into Pharaoh's house.

Immediately upon entering Egypt, Sarah's great beauty was noticed and she was taken to Pharaoh as a "gift." Even though no harm was done to her, the Sages taught that this was a trial of the faith of Abraham and Sarah (Midrash Tanchuma).

We can imagine that the trial must have been greater for Sarah than for Abraham, since her honor and her person were at stake. If so, we may ask why did Hashem, Whose ways are totally just and righteous, see fit to subject her to such a terrifying experience?

Many generations later, there was a similar episode when Esther was taken to be a wife of King Achashveirosh. Her uncle Mordechai, the leader of the Sanhedrin at the time, realized that Hashem would subject a righteous woman like Esther to such an experience only if it was required by an overall plan, out of which would come some enormous benefit to the people (see Rashi on Esther 2: 11). Thus Mordechai went daily to the gate of the king's palace to inquire about Esther, waiting expectantly for Hashem's plan to unfold. And, of course, in time it became clear to everyone that Hashem had positioned Esther exactly where she would need to be in order to thwart the machinations of the wicked Haman.

Here also, we may assume that the incident of Sarah's abduction must have been part of Hashem's master plan to accomplish a good purpose . We may further speculate that the benefit realized from the experience was very great, commensurate with the very distressing nature of the experience for Sarah and Abraham. But what was it? In the short term , we know the outcome. Pharaoh was stricken with severe plagues, which protected Sarah's honor, and was only too eager to give her back to Abraham. He also gave Abraham a sizable gift to assuage Sarah's offended feelings, making Abraham very wealthy as a result.

More importantly, however, this incident set a great example to all of Egypt. Everyone heard about the harsh punishment Pharaoh received for his unsuccessful attempt to impose himself on an unwilling Hebrew woman . This was a lesson that the Egyptian people would not soon forget.

Rashi comments in Parashas Pinchas (Bamidbar 26:5) , that the other nations scoffed at the Jews' scrupulousness in recording their lineage. "While they were in servitude , the Egyptians had control over their bodies. Surely they would also have exercised control over their wives. " Therefore , says Rashi , the Torah adds the letters yud and hei to the names of all of the families listed in Parashas Pinchas , a reference to one of Hashem 's names, as a sign that He Himself testified to the purity of their lineage.

This is truly remarkable. Why would the notoriously licentious Egyptians restrain themselves from taking advantage of their

Grieving & Healing

power over the Jewish women? It must be that the lesson of Pharaoh's punishment for his attempt to abuse the honor of a Hebrew woman had left such an indelible impression on the Egyptian character that even hundreds of years later, no Egyptian would allow such an idea even to enter his mind .

We may assume that this was the fruit of Hashem's "master plan" that made Sarah's distress worthwhile: In spite of the abject slavery in which the Egyptians held the Jews for two hundred and ten years , the memory of Pharaoh's punishment afforded Jewish women complete and absolute protection from any harm.

This story contains a powerful lesson for all of us. Whenever we undergo any kind of difficult experience, we must strengthen our faith in Hashem's goodness and believe that His master plan required us to endure that difficulty in order to accomplish something worthwhile . We should remember that, even though the benefits of Sarah's trial were not realized until several hundred years later, the result was nonetheless of incalculable importance. It is only because of the lesson Pharaoh learned from his encounter with Sarah that we can say that we are directly descended from our fathers Abraham, Isaac and Jacob.

March 2014, Comments at Hindy's 10th Yahrtzeit

Binyomin's Consolation of Yaakov

The *Navi Yeshayahu* (54:12) predicted and prophesied what was to be Hashem's consolation of the Jewish People after the Churban Bais Hamikdash: "I will make your windows of jewels and your gates of carbuncle stones."

This biblical prophesy of Nechama, one of the seven *Haftaros* of consolation, the *Shiva'ah DeNechemtah* is discussed in the *Gemorah Bava Basra* (75a)

> "This was a subject of disagreement between two *Malachim*: Malach Gavriel and Malach Michael, while some say the argument was between two rabbis, Reb Yehuda and Reb Chizkiya, the sons of Reb Chiya. One said this refers to the 'Shoham' stone, and the other says it refers to the 'Yashpeh' stone.' So the Almighty said, let it be both of them."

It is quite rare to find a disagreement between *Malachim* about interpreting a prophetic verse of consolation in the *Tanach*. And it is even more remarkable that Hashem's intervention was needed to decide the outcome. This would certainly seem to imply that Isaiah's prophecy is very significant and critical with respect to the future consolation of our nation.

The *Gemorah* explained Isaiah's prophesy that Hashem will console the Jewish People after being banished into *Golus* through the Yashpeh Stone which was one of 12 stones mounted on the *Choshen Mishpat*, the breastplate worn by

Grieving & Healing

Aharon Hakohein when he entered the *Kodesh Kodoshim* as a remembrance before Hashem. Each precious gem of the *Choshen* represented one of the twelve sons of Yaakov. The last of the *Choshen's* gems was the "Yashpeh" stone and Rabbeinu Bechaya cites a *Midrash* in *Parshas Tetzaveh* (28:20) which connects the Yashpeh stone with the Tribe of Binyamin.

This all begs the question: How does Biyomin's Yashpeh Stone on the *Choshen Mishpat* bring about consolation?

We see that the Torah makes a veiled reference to Binyomin's powers of consolation; in *Parshas Mikeitz*, (44:29) Yaakov Avinu states that if Binyomin were to go down to Mitzrayim and will not be returned to him *"then you will have brought down my hoariness in evil to the grave."* Rashi explains,

> "Now that Binyomin is next to me *"I am consoled through him"* over the death of his mother Rachel and over the death of his brother Yosef. So that if this one (Binyomin) were to die, it would seem to me that the three of them died on the same day."

Yet, this Rashi is curious, as the Torah recorded earlier"(37:35) that Yaakov Avninu refused to be consoled over Yosef's death:

> *"All his sons and all his daughters arose to comfort him, but he refused to comfort himself".*

Yaakov Avinu continued to grieve the entire twenty-two years of Yosef's absence, and he refused to accept any words of comfort and consolation. Yet, we see later in *Parshas Mikeitz*, that Binyomin seems to be able to console, Yaakov Avinu, a man who refused to be consoled.

Grieving & Healing

So we are left with a burning question: how exactly, did Binyomin console his inconsolable father Yaakov?

Binyomin's Silence

What makes this paradox even more curious, is that the Torah does not record Binyomin of ever speaking. He is literally silent when Yaakov Avinu debates with Reuvein and Yehuda whether to send him to Egypt or not, and he's even silent when wrongfully accused of stealing Yosef's goblet when his brothers accused him of being a thief, the son of a thief. (*"You stole the goblet, and your mother stole Lavan's idols."*) Binyomin was silent. He's not recorded in the Torah as having said a word.

The Torah does not give us any clues as to what *words* Binyomin *said* to his father to console his father. So how are we to discern the mystery of how Binyomin consoled his father when there are no words quoted to him, and there are no words attributed to him?

Binyomin's Pain & Anguish Over Yosef[11]

Further, we see in Parshas Vayigash (43:30) Binyomin's enormous pain and agony and loneliness over the tragedy of his brother Yosef, that he named each of his ten sons for a different aspect of Yoseif's being torn away from him.

Rashi, quoting Chazal (Tanchuma), tells us that Yosef and Binyamin actually had a dialogue that precipitated Yosef's crying.

---

11. Inspired by Rabbi Danny Korobkin

Grieving & Healing

Yosef asked Binyamin: "*Do you have a maternal brother?*"

Binyamin answered, "*I had one, but I don't know where he is.*" (Note that he did not say that my brother is deceased, just that he's missing.)

Yosef: "*Do you have any children?*"

Binyamin: "*I have ten sons.*"

Yosef: "*What are their names?*"

Binyamin then gave him the names.

Yosef asked, "*And what do these names mean?*"

Binyamin: "*All these names are after my brother and all that befell him.*"

Binyamin then proceeded to explain the ten names to Yosef (Rashi's source for the explanation of the 10 names is the Gemorah Sotah (36b)):

i. The first son, Bela, "because Yosef was ("*nivl'a*") "swallowed" up among the nations.

ii. The 2nd son, Becher, because he was his mother's firstborn (Rachel's "*b'chor*").

iii. The 3rd son, Ashbel, because Hashem made him a captive (a contraction of "*sh'va'o ell*"),

iv. The 4th son, Gaira, because he was a ("*Gair*") traveler or sojourner in a foreign land.

v. The 5th son, Na'aman, because he was ("*Na'im*") very pleasant

vi. The 6th son, Aichi, because he was my brother

("*Achi*" means my brother).

vii. The 7th son, Rosh, because he was my chief ("*Rosh*" means head or leader)

viii. The 8th son, Muppim, because he studied from the mouth of my father ("*Peh*").

ix. The 9th son, Chuppim,, because he did not see my wedding canopy (the "*Chuppah*"), nor did I see his.

x. The 10th son, Ard, because he descended among the nations ("*Yarad*" is the root "to go down").

The Maharal observed that of these ten names, five (Becher, Na'aman, Echi, Rosh, Muppim) described Binyomin's perceptions of Yosef's greatness, while the other five (Bela, Ashbel, Gera, Chuppim, Ard) described Biymonin's perceptions of the tragedies that befell Yosef. This contrast of Yosef's greatness and his mishaps only amplified the tragedy of his life and the intense pain that his brother Binyomin carried with him these 22 years regarding it. Binyamin missed his older brother Yosef so much and so intensely that he named every one of his 10 sons after Yosef.

And by revealing to Yosef the names of his 10 sons, Binyamin hinted that he was aware that Yosef wasn't killed by an animal, as his brothers told Yaakov Avniu. Binyamin knew very well the treachery that his brothers dealt Yosef, and to his father Yaakov. Imagine the resentment and distance that must have existed between Binyamin and his brothers. Imagine how lonely and isolated Binyomin was: he didn't have his mother Rachel in his life, he didn't have his big brother Yosef in his life,

Grieving & Healing

and he couldn't really have a normal relationship with any of his other brothers - since he knew the secret of *Mechiras Yosef*.

We also see that Binyomin is himself a tragic personality, having lost 5 of his 10 sons. The census done in *Parshas Pinchos*, which lists the heads of the tribal households, names only five of Binyomin's sons, yet we know that Binyomin had ten sons, who were among the 70 "souls" that descended to Egypt. Rashi brings a Medrash in the name of Rabbi Moshe ha-Darshan that Binyamin's offspring were predestined for tragedy; that is, when he was born to our Matriarch Rachel, and she lay dying in childbirth, Rachel named him "Ben Oni"-- "the child of mourning" and this name was a prophetic reference to the loss of Binyomin's 5 sons."

One can only marvel how such a tragic figure like Binyomin, a Ben Oni, a man predestined for the tragedy of bereavement, a man obsessed with his brother's tragedy, could possibly have any room within him to console his father.

Shevet Binyomin's Yashpeh Stone

Enter the *Yashpeh* Stone: Rabbeinu Bechaya cites a Midrash which connects the Yashpeh stone with the Tribe of Binyamin. Yashpeh, explains the Midrash, is a contraction of the words "yesh" and "peh" - "has a mouth"; it was chosen to represent Binyamin because its name reflects a praiseworthy trait displayed by him.

> "Binyamin knew that his brothers had sold Yosef into slavery, yet he did not reveal their shameful deed to their father, Yaakov. Although Binyamin had serious misgivings

about whether he should withhold this information from his father (which are reflected in the different colors of the jasper (consisting of red, black and green)) he could not foresee how Yaakov would react to such information, so he overcame his desire to reveal the secret. In the end he controlled himself, stopped himself, and did not reveal what he knew. The word "Yashpeh" may also be read, by rearranging the vowel marks, as 'Yesh Peh' -- 'there is a mouth.' Even though Binyamin was able to tell his father about his brothers' conduct -- 'he had a mouth' -- he refrained from doing so."

Rabbeinu Bachye, Shemos 28:15, from Midrash Bereishit Rabba 71:5.

Although Binyamin was aware that his brothers sold Yosef into slavery, he did not reveal their actions to his father. Binyamin also knew to keep his silence when the goblet was found in his possession. For these reasons, the Yashpeh Stone was associated with Binyamin.

If Binyamin was being lauded for his silence, why was the gem called "Yashpeh" - "has a mouth"? Should the more appropriate name not be *"Ain Peh"* - "has no mouth"? What trait did Binyamin exhibit through his silence?

Binyamin's loss of his only maternal brother at the hands of his paternal brothers was a highly traumatic experience for him. The only one to whom he could convey his feelings was his elderly father Yaakov, yet he refrained from doing so. By assigning the Yashpeh as the gem to represent Binyamin the Torah is attesting to the fact that Binyomin's abstinence from

Grieving & Healing

discussing his brother's fate to his father was not a result of his inability to divulge the information due to his trauma. On the contrary, "*Yesh Peh*", his ability to converse about the issue was indeed intact. Although it might have been of great emotional benefit for Binyamin to discuss the matter with his father, he remained selfless, as the knowledge that the pain his father would receive when enlightened as to his sons' actions would not permit Binyamin to speak.

Binyamin inherited the trait of discretion from his mother Rachel and passed in on to his descendants Shaul Hamelech and Esther Hamalkah, as the Gemara notes in Megillah (13b). Thus Binyomin's mother Rachel did not reveal Lavan's plot to exchange her for Leah under the Chuppah; Binyomin's descendant Shaul HaMelech did not prematurely reveal the fact that he had been crowned king of Israel; and Binyomin's descendant Esther HaMalkah did not reveal her origin to King Achashveirosh until Mordechai HaYeHudi instructed her to.

This acute sensitivity and selflessness to protecting others from pain, even at great personal sacrifice, stems from Binyamin's perfection of his discretion. And therein lies the genius of his ability to console his father properly.

A person who has endured a terribly traumatic experience very often is unable to discuss it with others for fear that discussing it will cause him to relive the painful experience. The person in trauma is in fear that the listener will not be tolerant, in fear that the listener will not be understanding, in fear that the listener will not be patient with the the Avel's grief and slow healing process, and fear that the listener might even be judgmental. Overcoming this fear and conversing

167

with a person who truly cares about him, and demonstrates discretion, helps ease the burden of the trauma.

Staying within our own space and not invading the space of others is the key to this powerful sound of silence. Speech is the area through which we have the greatest difficulty in focusing upon the sensitivities of others. All too often we speak up because of the benefit we derive from what we are saying, but fail to realize the damage we do to others with the content, with the decibel level and even verbosity of our speech.

In fact, being silent in the right place shows tremendous sensitivity, an important component in consoling others. In Halacha, when one goes to pay a Shiva call to be Menachem Aveleim, one is to remain silent until the Avel starts the conversation.

Binyomin displayed a great sensitivity and longing for kinship, to have that relationship with the brother he never had. This is why, when it was time for Hashem to console Binyomin's tribe with the ultimate blessings at the end of the Torah, Hashem tells Binyamin: Because you were deprived of your brother for the sake of the formation of Klal Yisrael, and because you showed discretion and wisdom and held your tongue to protect your father from pain and because you consoled him, I will console you by naming you the *"Yedid Hashem,"* Hashem's beloved friend, as Shevet Binyamin is called in Parshas V'zos HaBracha (33:12).

I promise you, says Hashem, you will never be alone ever again, Binyamin. The Holy of Holies, my place of resting of the Divine Presence, will lie in your portion of Eretz Yisrael. It is

Grieving & Healing

where the Divine Presence "will hover over for the whole day, and dwell amidst your shoulders." Says Hashem: No longer will you be lonely; I will be your friend, I will be your brother forever.

May we merit to always have our greatest Yedid, HKB"H, resting among us again, speedily in our days! On the 2nd day of Rosh Chodesh Adar II Monday March 3, 2014, we will commemorate the 10th Yahrtzeit of Hindy. *Bilah HaMoves Lanetzach, Umacha Hashem Elokim Dimah Meyal Kol Ponim* - May He swallow up death forever; may Hashem wipe away tears from every face (Isaiah 25:8) *T'hei Nishmasa Tzrurah B'tzror Ha'chaim.*

… Grieving & Healing

March 2015, Comments at Hindy's 11th Yahrtzeit

"Vayidom Aharon" the Sounds of Silence

This week, on Friday Rosh Chodesh Adar, we will commemorate the 11th Yahrtzeit of Hindy. This week, we were blessed with a Mazal Tov of our daughter Tali's engagement to Yechiel Hertz. The overlapping of these two events in our lives, caused me to reflect on the words of Shlomo Hamelech in Koheles [Ecclesiastes]: *"Dor Holech, VeDor Ba"* - A generation goes and a generation comes. *VeZarach HaShemes, Uva Hashemesh* - The sun rises and the sun sets. And I paraphrase Shlomo Hamelech: "To everything there is a season: a time to be born, and a time to die; a time to plant, and a time to pluck up that which is planted; a time to break down, and a time to build up; A time to weep, and a time to laugh; a time to mourn, and a time to dance." This is that kind of week.

Eighth Day[12]

The Torah in *Sefer Vayikra* 9:1 reports the day that *Aharon HaKohein's* 2 sons Nadav & Avihu died, that day was: *"Va Yehi Bayom HaShemini"* "And it was on the eighth day..."

To which eighth day is the Torah referring? The Torah is discussing the "eighth day" after the previous seven, during which the Jewish people performed the *Shivas Yimei Ha-Miluim* - the Seven Days of Inauguration Offerings. It was a

---

12. Inspired by Rabbi Yissochor Frand

Grieving & Healing

"*Chanukas HaBayis*" [inaugural dedication], so to speak, for the *Mishkan* [Tabernacle], with *Moshe Rabbeinu* acting as the *Kohen Gadol* [High Priest]. The "eighth day" referred to in the *Pasuk* was the day when Aharon took over from Moshe, and the *Mishkan* began functioning in its normal way with the Kohanim performing the services.

It is peculiar that the Torah refers to this occasion as the "eighth" day. It was really the "first" day. The first seven days were merely a dry-run rehearsal. Every day, they put up the *Mishkan* and then took it down, and the *Shechina*, the Divine Presence, did not rest within it. But this day, was the real "Day One" of the functioning of the *Mishkan*, when the *Shechina* came down from heaven, [9:23] yet the *Torah* insists on calling it the "eighth day". The Torah emphasizes the previous seven days nonetheless, even calling the whole *Parsha* "*Shemini*" (meaning eighth). What message is the Torah giving us?

It Should Have Been a Day of Joy

It should have been a day of joy. Klal Yisroel had completed the *Mishkan*. For seven days Moshe had made preparations for its consecration. Now on the eighth day – the first of Nissan, the service of the sanctuary was about to begin. The *Gemorah* in *Megillah* 10b says that it was in heaven the most joyous day since creation.

No doubt, *Aharon HaKohein* must have woken up that morning thinking, "This will be the best day ever. It simply can't get any better." It was opening day at the *Mishkan*. He and his sons would be installed as the *Kohanim* - Priests and would initiate the very first service in the history of this magnificent edifice.

Grieving & Healing

The nation was there, the elders were gathered, and with the encouragement of his younger brother Moshe, Aharon was ready to begin.

Can you imagine the pride that Aharon must have felt when he was appointed *Kohein Gadol*? Here he was, born and raised a slave in Egypt, yet he found himself appointed the highest religious authority of the Jewish people. And at the same time that Aharon was appointed *Kohen Gadol* his sons were appointed to the very important office of *Kohanim* to serve the Jewish people and to serve God. When Aharon woke up on the morning – on the eighth and final day of the inaugural ceremony–he probably told himself "it doesn't get any better than this."

It should have been a day of joy; and then tragedy struck. The two elder sons of Aharon "offered a strange fire, that had not been commanded,". The fire from heaven that should have consumed the sacrifices consumed them as well. They died.

The Gemorah in Sanhedrin reports: "*Shnei Chutin Shel Aish Yatzu MiBais Kodesh HaKadashim*" two shafts of fire issued from the chamber of the Holy of Holies, "*VeNechleku LeArba VeNichnisu BeChutmo Shel Zeh, Ushnayim BeChutmo Shel Zeh, VeSarpham*" - and the flames divided into four, two entered the nostrils of Nadav's nose and two entered into the nostrils of Avihu's nose, and tragically burned them to death.

Aharon's joy instantly incinerated and turned to mourning. It went up in flames, literally. Aharon then experienced the absolute worst nightmare of any parent – the loss of his children before his very eyes, and in front of the entire nation. What

Grieving & Healing

began as the best day of his life suddenly was transformed into the worst.

Most of could only imagine how we would respond at such a sight: unbearable pain, searing horror, grief, agony, screaming out in indescribable anguish. Maybe even anger.

How did Aharon react? Did he scream, did he sob uncontrollably? Did he challenge God and storm out of the Mishkan defiantly? No. In the case of Aharon, all it says is *Vayidom Aharon*, Aharon was silent, still.

The word used to describe his stillness is *Vayidom*. It is, for me, among the most powerful and compelling words in all of Torah. Four letters. Painfully short. Dramatically onomatopoetic. Vayido*m*. Three syllables ending with a slamming shut of your lips. Almost as if an action suggestive of the forcing of silence upon oneself. Vayido*m*.

Vayidom Aharon, "And Aharon was silent." The man who had been Moshe's spokesman could no longer speak. It was as if words turned to ash in his mouth.

What Could Aharon Have Said?[13]

Vayidom Aharon, "And Aharon was silent." The *Medrash* says that this verse implies that Aharon really did have something to say, but that he held back. He became silent. What did Aharon want to say? The *Medrash* gives a very cryptic answer: He wanted to say *"U'vayom Ha'shemini Yimol Besar Orlaso"* *"On the eighth day the flesh of his foreskin shall be circumcised."* [Vayikra 12:13]

---
13. Inspired by Rabbi Yissochor Frand

Grieving & Healing

What is the meaning of this enigmatic *Medrash*? The *Shemen HaTov* answers by quoting a *Gemarah* [*Niddah* 31b]: The *Gemarah* asks why *Milah* [circumcision] takes place on the eighth day - why not circumcise the baby boy immediately at birth? The *Gemarah* answers that *Milah* occurs on the eighth day: "*Shelo Yihu Kulam Semaichim VeAviv VeImo Atzavim*" - so that we will not have a situation where everyone is happy and the parents of the child are sad.

The *Gemora* answers that when a woman has a male child, she becomes impure and forbidden to her husband for seven days. If the circumcision was performed on the seventh day, the guests would be rejoicing while the parents, the central figures at the celebration, would still be sad. On the eighth day, the mother has had the opportunity to immerse in a *Mikvah* and become permitted to her husband, allowing them to also enjoy the occasion.

Based on the *Gemorah*'s reasoning, we may explain that Aharon was the primary participant in the joy of the inauguration of the *Mishkan*, in which he served as *Kohen Gadol*. After seeing the lengths to which the *Torah* goes to ensure that the parents are able to be happy at their son's circumcision, Aharon was bothered that he lost two of his children on the day which was supposed to be so dear to him.

The *Shemen HaTov* explains that Aharon could have argued with Hashem. "Granted my sons did something wrong, they deserved to be punished - but do not execute Your Judgment on them today, of all days! After all, we learn that *Milah* is done on the eighth day because You are sensitive not to place a damper on a joyous occasion." However, Aharon held his

Grieving & Healing

peace and kept quiet. "*Vayidom Aharon*" Aharon remained like a stone.

Aharon's Reward (A Death Penalty Mitzvah?)

Rashi describes Aharon's incredible reward for remaining silent and faithful in the face of profound adversity. Immediately after the Torah informs us of Aharon's reaction, the Torah says that Hashem taught Aharon the law that a *Kohein* may not drink wine when he comes to perform the *Avodah*. Rashi explains that this was Aharon's reward for his silence. In other words, according to Rashi, *HaKadosh Baruch Hu* gave Aharon special *Chizuk* for his reaction to his sons' deaths by speaking to Aharon alone and not, as He usually did, by speaking to Moshe and Aharon together or to Moshe alone.

The question that arises, however, is that the special *Mitzvah* which Hashem teaches Aharon basically comes to warn the *Kohein* doing the *Avodah* that if he comes to the *Bias HaMikdash* after drinking wine, he will die! A *Mitzvah* with a death penalty as its punishment.

Is this the *Chizuk* that one gives to a person who has just lost two sons? "Be careful or else you and your other two sons will die too"? What is the meaning behind Rashi's comment that this special *Mitzvah* was Aharon's reward for his silence?

Ironically, Hashem Tells Moshe to Be Quiet

The *Gemorah Menachos* 29b provides that when *HaKadosh Baruch Hu* showed Moshe the true greatness of *R' Akiva*, Moshe asked *HaKadosh Baruch Hu*, "If You have such a great person, why don't You give the Torah through him?" *Hakadosh*

Grieving & Healing

Baruch Hu responded, "*Shtok*, be silent!" [*Shtok; Kach Alsah b'Machshavah l'Fanai*]. Moshe continued, asking to see *R' Akiva's* reward for his Torah. *HaKadosh Baruch Hu* showed Moshe the markets of Rome, where *R' Akiva's* flesh was being weighed and sold. Moshe challenged, *Zu Torah V' Zu Sechorah* "This is the Torah and this is its reward?!" *HaKadosh Baruch Hu* again responded, "*Shtok*! This is what I have decided"

Moshe Rabbeinu was able to comprehend the word of Hashem face to face "*B'aspaklarya Ha'Me'irah*," with a clarity akin to a clear lens that allows bright light to shine through. What kind of response is "*Shtok* to such a great man with such great clarity into Hashem!"? How does that answer (silence) the question?

Rather, *HaKadosh Baruch Hu* was teaching Moshe - that there are things that one can understand only if one sees the entire picture. And this can only be done when one is silent... Because when one speaks, one concentrates only on what he's saying, ignoring the surroundings. *Shtikah* allows one to evaluate his surroundings and to see the entire picture.

R' Akiva teaches us this lesson in *Pirkei Avos* as well *Seyag Lachochmah, Shtikah*, Silence leads one to wisdom; *Shtikah* is a guarantee for *Chochmah*, because through *Shtikah* one is able to perceive the entire picture.

This was the greatness of Aharon's silence. His silence didn't represent emotional coldness, for according to the *Ramban* he certainly cried bitterly over the death of his two sons. Rather, Aharon had the *Ma'alah* (positive trait) of *Shtikah*, which let him see the entire picture, enabling him to accept the deaths of his sons with tranquility and love for Hashem.

Grieving & Healing

One who has the quality of *Shtikah* can discover great *Sodos* (secrets), because the whole point

of a *Sod* is that it remains a *Sod*. Aharon's silence demonstrated his mastery of the trait of *Shtikah*, and thus, his unique ability to uncover *Sodos*.

As he began his career in the *Bais HaMikdash*, where he would be privy to the *Sod* of Creation and to all sorts of other *Sodos*, *HaKadosh Baruch Hu* warns him not to drink wine, because "*Nichnas Yayin Yatza Sod*, When wine comes in, secrets come out." According to the *Klei Yakar*, this commandment is not a warning that Aharon may die too, but rather an emphasis of Aharon's intimacy with *Sod*, an emphasis of Aharon's intimacy with Hashem.

We now understand how this *Halacha* served as a source of incredible *Chizuk* to *Aharon HaKohein*, essentially praising him as the paradigm of "*Sod Hashem li'y'reiav*, Hashem shares His secrets with those who fear Him" (Tehillim 25:14).

Hashem speaks directly and only to him, and says, "don't drink wine when you come close to Me", no mind-altering of any sorts, chemical or conceptual.

When you are so, so close, that agony and ecstasy fade away into the deeper silence, that's where you'll find Me. That's where you can maintain *Yichud* with me. That's where you can experience that intimacy with *Hashem*.

Perhaps by Being Quiet, Aharon Was Actually Speaking Volumes. The "Sounds of Silence."

Va'yidom Aharon, he fell silent, he was still. What was the nature of Aharon's silence? After all, there are many different forms and causes of silence. There is the comforting and supportive silence of companionship. There is the awkward and uncomfortable silence between conversations. There is the peaceful and serene silence of a moment of tranquility. And there is the silence of shock, speechlessness, and astonishment.

The subject of deep silence is one that often makes people, particularly in our day and age, rather uncomfortable. Silence can be disconcerting. Many of us associate silence with awkward pauses in conversation. Many of us run from silence, because in total silence, we're left with only our own thoughts and worries and insecurities nagging at us. For others among us, silence is the experience of sheer terror. Silence, particularly deep stillness, reminds some of us of death, of hopelessness and passivity, of the absence of life and possibility.

But there's another aspect of stillness and silence that few of us have taken the time to consider: that when we welcome moments of stillness and silence into our experience fearlessly, it can be incredible, restorative, the very opposite of insecurity and fear, the very opposite of death's finality.

Some of my most powerful and meaningful moments of healing after the tragedy of Hindy's death came from friendship and love that was communicated - in silence. The embrace of a friend who cares. The hug. The grasping of a hand. The squeeze on my shoulder when I was losing it under my *Tallis*. The smile. The looking into the eyes of the other. An expression of caring and concern; a reaching out from the heart, a gesture of hope. It is the world of sacred connection. It is the world of silence.

Grieving & Healing

You, my friends: it was your presence, your silence, your gentle eyes, that were the safest sanctuaries that my tormented soul could confide with. Even for just a moment, I was able to be myself, vulnerable and hurt, with you. My tragedy, as poorly expressed by my words, found no better rest than in your arms, in your easy eyes, and in your space.

After Hindy died, A friend in the Shul took me for a walk in Hancock Park every Shabbos morning where we just walked, without speaking. We walked a mile, then two, yet there were no words exchanged. Something beyond words kept us quiet because that was sacred space. There was something between, that words would only violate, if expressed. Our walks often changed me. The silence of a brother helping out a brother in pain, that consoled me.

I would like to suggest, that silence is not necessarily, the absence of words. Silence can happen when we catch our breath, in between speaking. Silence itself can be a form of crying out. Indeed, the *Kotzker Rebbe* described a certain type of silence that represents yelling quietly. *Dovid Ha'Melech* in *Tehillim* (65) tells God, *Lecha Dumiya Tehila,* "silence to you is praise." Elsewhere, in *Tehillim* (62) he tells us: *Ach El Elokim, Dumiyah Nafshi Mimenu Yeshuasi* - "My soul waits in silence only for God; from Him comes my salvation."

Sometimes more can be said with silence than could ever be articulated with words. It wasn't that Aharon had nothing to say and therefore he was silent. Rather, he used a shattering and stunning silence to say so much about himself and about his relationship and faith in *Hashem*. In fact, the *Rambam* quotes a reading of the *Targum Onkelos* that translates the word "*Vayidom*" as *U'shevach Aharon*, and Aharon praised *Hashem* through his silence. Aharon used silence to make a statement of faith in reacting to a horrific tragedy.

What Is the Message of Vayidom?

Curiously, the Torah does not say "*Vayishtok*" Aharon, the more conventional word used for silence, which may have been the more logical choice. Why does it use the term *Va'yidom*?

Perhaps we can draw insight from other instances where the word "*Vayidom*" is used.

During the *Yomim Noraim*, when we recite the *Nesaneh Tokef*: "*Uvashofar Gadol Yitakah, V'kol Demam'mah Dakah Yishama*" – the great shofar is sounded, and a whispered, small voice is heard.

The phrase "*Demam'mah*" as in *V'kol Demam'mah Dakah* comes from *Sefer Melachim Aleph*, the first book of Kings.

Eliyahu HaNavi, the prophet Elijah, who, during a time of great despondency journeyed to Mount Sinai, the very place where God thundered the Ten Commandments to all of Israel generations before, because *Eliyahu* wanted to hear the voice of God speaking to him personally. And the story describes how all these amazing forces of nature revealed themselves to *Elijah*: first, a great wind blasted the face of the mountain, shattering even the rocks on the cliffside. But, says the story, *Lo BaRuach*: God was not in the wind. Then, a great earthquake made the whole mountain tremble, but ...*Vlo B'ra'ash* ... God was not in the earthquake. Next a terrible fire swept everything into flames, but... *Lo B'esh*: God was not in the fire.

Grieving & Healing

And then finally, after all the fire and earth-shattering noise, *Eliyahu HaNavi* heard a *Kol Demamah Dakah*, a still, small voice. (1 Kings 19: 11-12) And in that still, small Voice, was God's Presence.

Note that the Hebrew for 'still small Voice:' *Kol Demamah Dakah* — the same word *Demamah/Domem*: meaning absolute Silence and stillness, the same stillness that Aharon showed at the death of his sons.

"Be'damayikh Chayii"

Perhaps we can say homilectically, that when we attend a *Bris Milah* and we chant the words of the *Navi Yechezkiel* (16:6): *Vayomar Lach Bedamayich Chayi Vaomar Lach Bedamayich Chayai* "Then I passed and I saw that you were rooted in your blood, and I said to you, 'by your blood shall you live'"

I always understood these words '*Be'damayikh Chayii*,' to mean 'by your blood shall you live,' because of the bloody sacrifices the Jews have forced to make for our God and our faith, we merited the covenantal gift of eternal life.

But perhaps we can now view the clause differently. Now that we have suffered unspeakable tragedies it seems to me that *Ezekiel*'s choice of word '*Damayikh*' comes not from the Hebrew *Dam*, blood, but rather from the Hebrew *Dom*, silence, as in '*Vayidom Aharon*' – and Aharon was silent.

Perhaps it is because we held back from battering the gates of heaven with our cries, because we swallowed our sobs and continued to pray and continued to learn and to build and to plant, because we utilized our energies not to weep over our past losses but rather to recreate our lives, that we continue to live and even to flourish.

And perhaps this explains the genius of the Torah reporting the day of the death of Nadav & Avihu and Aahon's response, "*VaYehi Bayom HaShemini*" "And it was on the eighth day...", making veiled reference to a *Bris Milah*; hence making reference to *Vayomar Lach Bedamayich Chayi Vaomar Lach Bedamayich Chayai*; shedding light into the *Kol Demamah Dakah*, and ultimately shedding light into the *Vayidom Aharon*.

Morai VeRabosai: it is in the silences between the notes, between the gasps of pain and anguish, between the noise we hear and the endless thoughts of our tormented minds, there, in those silent gaps, we can find the very powerful Voice of God! This was the *Demamah*, this was the silence, that Aharon showed us in his moment of tragedy. Hence the genius of the words *Vayidom Aharon*.

Without that still silence, the noise of this world can overwhelm us with grief and stress. That *Kol Demamah Dakah* lives within our very hearts. It's there, in the silent spaces between our words, between the very thoughts we think in our heart of hearts. When we, can transcend our pain and emulate *Aharon HaKohein* and *David Hamelech*, like *Eliyahu HaNavi* and learn to listen to the stillness within, and reach down into our core to find ourselves, in that, we find the context, we find the meaning, and we find the strength, and even the joy to be able to face the fierce noise of life itself.

That Silent stillness is always there for us, it's just beneath the surface, it's waiting for us to listen.

Grieving & Healing

Let's listen for our own *Kol Demamah Dakah*, and may it give us the strength to face this world, and to transform this world from noise to music, and from tragedy to joy.

Perhaps one day, we will merit the fulfillment of *David HaMelech's* phrase in of Tehillim: and no longer need to be silent, *"Lema'an yizamercha kavod 'V'lo Yidom,"* in order that my soul sing praises to You, God, and will NOT be silent!

Bilah HaMoves Lanetzach, Umacha Hashem Elokim Dimah Meyal Kol Ponim - May He swallow up death forever; may Hashem wipe away tears from every face (Isaiah 25:8) *T'hei Nishmasa Tzrurah B'tzror Ha'chaim.*

March 5, 2016, Broken Heart & Shattered Luchos, Comments of Baruch Cohen in Observance of the 12th Yahrtzeit of Hindy Cohen

Avinu Malkeinu: the Shoes of the Danube

Rabbi Moshe Weinberger, rav of the Aish Kodesh shul in Woodmere, Long Island, tells of a remarkable story that I would like to share with you before the Dvar Torah:

A Chassid asked his Rebbe: there are two lines in the prayers that are said on the holiest day of the year *Rosh Hashana* - the *Avinu Malkeinu* that seem to echo the same sentiment:

> *Avinu Malkeinu; Asei LeMaan Harugim Al Shem Kadshecha* - our Father, our King, act for the sake of those who were *murdered for Your Holy Name*;

followed by:

> *Avinu Malkeinu; Asei Lemaan Tevuchim Al Yechudecha* - our Father, our King, act for the sake of those *slaughtered for your Oneness.*

What's the difference between those who were *Harugim Al Shem Kadshecha* 'murdered for Your Holy Name' and those who were *Tevuchim Al Yechudecha* 'slaughtered for your Oneness?'

The Chassid answered:

"I am a Holocaust survivor. I lived in a small shtetl in Budapest, Hungary where, on the night of January 8, 1945 the Nazi division known as the Hungarian Arrow Cross

Grieving & Healing

Militiaman marched into my town, rounded up all of the Jews, approximately 100 people, to the banks of the Danube River. They lined us up, side by side, at the river's edge not far from the Hungarian Parliament building. We were ordered to take off our shoes, and were to be shot at the edge of the water so that our bodies would fall into the icy river and get carried away. The Nazis pulled the shoestrings out of our shoes, and used them to tie our helpless hands together before we were shot. They positioned us at the edge of the water, so that when one Jew would fall into the river, the dead body would pull the still-living victims with it. The killers faced us without mercy; and we faced our killers without blindfolds.

Then one of the Nazi commanders who was standing on the embankment of the river, lifted his machine gun at us and began to shoot, starting from the right side, moving to the left. All of us Jews raised our voices at once and cried out to G-d the sentence from the Torah that Jews say when sanctifying their lives in God's name: "*Shema Yisroel Hashem Elokeinu Hashem Achad!*" The ones on the right side of the line, were unable to complete the Shema and they only got mid-sentence "*Shema Yisroel Hashem...*", while those on the left side of the line, managed to say all of the words of the Shema before falling into the river. The Danube river was red with blood that day. All the bodies, tied together by shoelaces or rope or fate, would either sink or float away down the river. If the Nazis noticed that some of us Jews were still alive, they used us for target practice.

"Rebbeh" the Chassid said: "I survived that bloody brutal massacre, I passed out for a second or two but the ice cold water of the Danube in December revived me instantly. I remember coming to my senses and clearly realizing what had happened. Those Yidden on the right side who were killed instantly, were murdered by mid-sentence, they were *Harugim Al Shem Kadshecha* by the word: "Hashem" His holy name; while those on the left, who managed to finish the entire Shema all the way to the last word "*Echad*" they were *Tevuchim Al Yechudecha* they were slaughtered by his oneness."

Morai Verabosai, today in 2016, "*The Shoes on the Danube*" is a memorial in Budapest, Hungary, on the banks of the Danube River, there sit sixty pairs of shoes, the type worn in the 1940s, as a memorial to those slaughtered by the Nazis [PICTURE].

Every Yom Tov that I daven in this shul, and ascend to Duchen to do *Nesias Kapaim*, I and other Kohanim in this shul take off our shoes and leave them in a row up front, every time I see our shoes lined up, I'm reminded of the haunting scene of the *Shoes of the Danube*, and of those holy martyrs who were *Harugim Al Shem Kadshecha* 'murdered for Your Holy Name' and those who were *Tevuchim Al Yechudecha* 'slaughtered for your Oneness.

Broken

The Gemorah in Bava Basra 14a teaches us that: "*Luchos Ve'shivrey Luchos Munachim Be'Aron*" the whole Luchos (the tablets) and the broken Luchos nestled inside the *Aron Kodesh*, the Ark of the Covenant.

This seems strange. Why would Hashem place the broken tablets in the *Kodesh Kodoshim*? After all, these fragments were

Grieving & Healing

a constant reminder of the great moral failure of *Klal Yisroel*.

In *Parshas Eikev*, we read that after *Klal Yisroel* created an *Eigal HaZahav*, the Golden Calf, Moshe Rabbeinu smashed the stone tablets created by Hashem, engraved with the *Aseres Hadibros*, the Ten Commandments. Moshe Rabbeinu, outraged by the sight of an *Eigal HaZahav* erected by Klal Yisroel as a deity, smashed the stone tablets. He apparently felt that Klal Yisroel was undeserving of them, and that it would be inappropriate to give them this Divine gift.

On Yom Kippur, the holiest day of the year, the Kohein Godol would not perform the service with his usual golden garments, since gold was remotely reminiscent of the golden calf. Yet in this instance, throughout the entire year, the very symptom of the golden calf – the broken tablets – were stored in the *Kodosh Kodoshim*!

Why?

Broken Hearts; Shattered Luchos

The 16th century Kabbalistic work, *Reshis Chochmah*, teaches that the Ark is a symbol of the human heart. HaRav Eliyahu de Vidash of Tzfat:

> *"The human heart is the Ark, thus a person's heart must be full of Torah but simultaneously be a Broken Heart, a beaten heart. Only thus can it serve as a home for the Divine Presence. For it only dwells in broken vessels."*

The two sets of tablets in the Ark offer a striking metaphor. Namely, that brokenness and wholeness can coexist side by side, even in Judaism's holiest spot – in the heart of the holy Ark. *"Luchos Ve'shivrey Luchos Munachim Be'Aron"*

People experience brokenness in many ways. One way that many of us experience despair and crushing pain is through the death of a loved one, especially when life is cut short. Those of us who have passed through the 'Valley of Death' and wept through the 'Valley of Tears' those of us who have lost loved ones, know that we forever carry 'broken tablets' within us. Loss forever remains a part of us. We carry the aching loss, and for some of us, we carry pain in our hearts and minds forever. We carry our brokenness with us always. After a painful loss, life continues, but now differently than before. We move through life now with two sets of tablets. There are times of joy; there are very happy times. They are also encased in the same box; in the same heart.

The bereaved, and especially those that have suffered painful loss, often live their life with two compartments within one heart – the whole and the broken, side by side

We yearn for our lives to be whole, to experience a sense of unity and one-ness, but more often than we care to admit, that experience is elusive, evasive, unattainable. The intact tablets, pristine in their perfection, convey an image of completeness and wholeness that is at odds with our fragmentary experience. The image of the broken tablets offers a more accurate representation of our lives and our world.

Rising from the Ashes

Usually, we think of wholeness and brokenness as two diametrically opposed states of being. But that isn't necessarily so. Sometimes brokenness leads to wholeness to the point that without the broken pieces, there could be no whole.

There are moments when Hashem desires that we connect to Him as wholesome people, with clarity and a sense of fullness; there are yet deeper moments when He desires that we find Him in the shattered experiences of our lives.

As Rabbi YY Jacobson said:

> *"We hope and pray to always enjoy the "whole tablets," but when we encounter the broken ones, we ought not to run from them or become dejected by them; with tenderness we ought to embrace them and bring them into our "holy of holies," recalling the observation of the Kotzker Rebbe, "there is nothing more whole, than a broken heart.""*

What Moshe Rabbeinu accomplished with breaking the Luchos was the demonstration of the truth that holiness can be carved out from the very alienation of a person from Hashem. From the very turmoil of his or her psychological and spiritual brokenness, a new holiness can be discovered.

It is on this note that the Torah chooses to culminate its tribute to Moshe Rabbeinu' life. In its eulogy for Moshe, the Torah chooses this episode of smashing the tablets as *the* highlight and climax of Moshe's achievements. His greatest achievement? How about *Yetzias Mitzrayim* - his taking the Jews out of Egypt? Molding them into a people? *Krias Yam Suf* - the Splitting the

Red Sea? *Kabbalas HaTorah* - the receiving the Torah from G-d and transmitting it to humanity? Shepherding them for forty years in a wilderness? Yet, the Torah chooses this tragic and devastating episode of his shattering the tables to capture the zenith of Moshe Rabbeinu's life and as the theme with which to conclude the entire Torah.

Perhaps the greatest achievement of Moshe Rabbeinu was his ability to show humanity how we can take our brokenness and turn it into a *Kodesh Kodoshim*.

The Sages teach that the Holy Ark "carried those who carried it." When the priests "carried" the Ark, rather than feel its weight, the priests would feel energized and lifted up; the Ark miraculously "carried" them. So, too, our broken parts need not weigh us down. When we use our brokenness as a catalyst toward wholeness, our broken pieces lift us up and move us forward.

Turn to Nothing to Become Something

After my very being felt like it was dissolving after Hindy's death, I subsequently realized at one point in time that I was undergoing a kind of alchemy, a transmutation of self, that may one day invite and include something much more powerful than the pain I was going through. Of course, I would prefer to be a more relaxed superficial person with my daughter alive than to be imbued with a profound sense of mission. But in my spiritual journey beyond grief, I came to realize that within suffering, lies a form of greatness.

As Sherri Mandel, the author of *"The Blessings of a Broken*

Grieving & Healing

Heart" and of *"Resilience"* wrote:

> *"When we permit ourselves to enter the chaos, to stumble, to cry out, to surrender to our defenselessness, we may find that our pain leads us towards greater truths about our vulnerabilities, and our power in this world. Entering the chaos prepares us to receive a heightened clarity and wisdom as well as to engage in a more intimate relationship with Hashem."*

Dovid Hamelech's Tehillim 126 is a psalm of hope; in it's final lines, we recognize a deep connection between emptiness and formation.

> *HaZorim BeDimah BeRinah Yiktzoru* - Those who sow in tears will reap in song;
>
> *HaLoch Yelech Uvacha Nosei Meshech Hazorah* - Those who bear the measure of seed goes on his weeping;
>
> *Bo Yavo BeRinah Nosei Alumosav* - He shall surely come home with exultation, bearing his sheaves.

When it feels like the earth that supported you has been irreparably overturned, there is a divine promise in Dovid Hamelech's Tehillim that new seedlings will one day take root and grow. We are promised a harvest when it seems improbable, when we cannot fathom nor imagine growth.

Every seed has to disintegrate before it can grow into a fruit or vegetable. Every seed has to break apart to sprout. It has to surrender to the darkness of mystery in order to emerge. And therein lies the stunning truth of life, of grief, and of healing: the seed has to turn to nothing to become something.

How do we cope with fear and pain of nothingness or of brokenness? By realizing that a crucial aspect of resilience is the ability to allow the darkness, to surrender, to pause in the chaos of pain, to suspend our routine, to wait, to receive. We have to learn to stop, and allow the waves of pain to wash over us. Because once we are broken, then Hashem can be the Healer of the Broken Hearted as Dovid Hamelech calls the *Rofei LiShburei Lev*.

We dwell in a crucible of doubt and imbalance, of emptiness and anguish. One has to undergo the process of decomposition in order to be reborn. "*The things which hurt,*" Benjamin Franklin wrote, "*instruct.*" As Ryan Holiday, the author of *The Obstacle Is the Way: The Timeless Art of Turning Trials into Triumph* says: "What impedes us, can actually empower us."

To be able to contain this truth requires deep humility, faith in God, and surrender. It's almost impossible to believe that at the moment of destruction and dissolution, that rebirth is actually beginning. Yet it is said, that on Tisha Bav, Moshiach is born.

Cracked Pots & the Art of Kintsukuroi

A story is told about a man who owned two large pots. Each hung on the ends of a pole, which he carried every day on his shoulders to fill with water from the stream located at the end of the village. One of the pots was complete and always delivered a full portion of water; the other pot was cracked and arrived home each day only half full. Of course, the complete pot was proud of its accomplishments. It felt really good about

Grieving & Healing

itself. The poor cracked pot, on the other hand, was ashamed of its own imperfections; it was miserable that it could only do half of what it had been made to do. After years of what it perceived to be bitter failure, the humbled broken pot finally opened its heart to the man at the stream. "I hate myself," the cracked pot cried, "I am so useless and valueless. What purpose does my existence have when each day I leak out half of my water? I am such a loser!"

The man smiled and said:

"Did you notice that there are flowers on your side of the path, but not on the other pot's side? I have always known about your flaw, so I planted flower seeds on your side of the path. Every day while we walk back from the stream, you have the opportunity to water them. "For years I have been able to pick these beautiful flowers to decorate our home. Without you being just the way you are, broken, cracked and imperfect, we would have never created this beauty together."

In fact, to build on this profound idea, the Japanese employ a method for repairing broken ceramics with a special lacquer mixed with gold, silver, or platinum. It's called Kintsugi (or Kintsukuroi) where the damage to a ceramic is not just mended and hidden, but the cracks are filled with gold and literally become the highlights of the piece. They symbolize an event that took place in the life of the object, much like events that happen in the lives of humans that cannot be reversed but leave us forever marked. Instead of seeing these events as something shameful to be hidden or disguised, the Japanese lovingly and compassionately transform the flaws into an exquisite piece of art that usually becomes more valuable than

Grieving & Healing

the original piece.

This week, on Friday Rosh Chodesh Adar, we will commemorate the 12th Yahrtzeit of Hindy. We will never forget Hindy.

We feel diminished and broken by her loss, for she was a beacon illuminating our family with a special light. I will continue to declare it every day, and especially on the day of her Yahrtzeit.

Hollywood screenwriter Robert Avrech, also a fellow bereaved parent, put it best, in describing his intense yearning for his deceased son Ariel's *Neshamah* after years of bereavement - which I will apply and adapt to mine to Hindy's: "*Contrary to all logic, as time passes, our memories of Hindy have become more vivid. The images of every stage of her life are easier to evoke in all nuance and detail. This is a mixed blessing since it intensifies our longing for her smile, her steadfastness, her intelligence and kindness. Yet the enrichment of memory strengthens her role in our family as a luminous spirit, guiding us in the corporeal world. Her goodness, her modest piety are a constant reminder of what we should all strive for in our lives. Indeed, Hindy's absence has been transformed into a deeply felt presence.*"

We always think about her, but we continue on, with the "second set of *Luchos*" even after our first set was broken and shattered. When we feel that our "set of *Luchos*" are shattered, we need only open our hearts to receive Hashem's gift of a "second set of *Luchos*," the belief that joy can, and will, find a place in our lives again, with *Luchos* that will never be broken.

Bilah HaMoves Lanetzach, Umacha Hashem Elokim Dimah Meyal Kol Ponim - May He swallow up death forever; may Hashem wipe away tears from every face (Isaiah 25:8) *T'hei*

Grieving & Healing

Nishmasa Tzrurah B'tzror Ha'chaim.

Grieving & Healing

Shedding Tears over the Deaths of the Sons on Aharon Hakohein - Comments of Baruch Cohen in Observance of the 13th Yahrtzeit of Hindy Cohen

Hindy's 13th yahrtzeit which will be observed on Monday Rosh Chodesh Adar 2-27-2017 - Adar 1, 5777.

Rav Akiva Eiger's Pure Dove

HaGaon Rabbi Akiva Eger (1761 – 1837) was an outstanding *Talmud Chochom*, an extraordinary Torah scholar, an influential *Posek HaDor* and foremost leader of European Jewry during the early 19th century.

He married Glicky Margolis (who was then 16 years old) in 1778 and had 4 children together. After 18 years of marriage, Glicky got sick and tragically died. Rabbi Akiva Eger was 34 years old at the time and was absolutely devastated and distraught.

Shortly thereafter, his deceased wife's sister and brother-in-law, saw that Rabbi Akiva Eger was in need of a life's partner and offered him their daughter's hand in marriage (Breinda Feivelman who was then 16 years old). His four children were still unmarried at the time.

In a most powerful and remarkable letter (*Michtivei Rabbi Akiva Eiger, 109*) Rabbi Akiva Eger wrote a response to the Rabbonim who were asked to make the marriage suggestion for Ms. Breindel Feivelman to him. He respectfully declined the offer for the time being, explaining that he was unable to

Grieving & Healing

move forward until he first came to grips with the tragedy of his loss [Rabbi Yosef Tropper translated large segments of this incredibly powerful letter in his book "The Aishes Chayil Song" which you can get on Amazon. Rabbi Akiva Eger wrote:

> "How can I answer you (regarding the proposed match)? My senses are confused, I cannot concentrate on anything.... 'I firstly must state that I find this proposal to be insulting to my in-laws who are mourning the loss of their daughter as well."

Still, he reacted with astonishment to the thought of a match being proposed so soon after the loss of:

> "the wife of my youth, my pure dove, with whom Hashem blessed me ... She walked a son and a daughter together with me down the aisle with joy and happiness ... Who will I share my worries with and receive comfort, who will look after me and care for me ... Who knew her righteousness more than I? Many times we were up in animated discussions about the topic of Yiras Shamayim until the middle of the night."

Rav Akiva Eiger did not hesitate to bare the depth of his despair, which rendered him, as yet, unfit for marriage:

> "As you can see, I am a broken man, in a dark world (See, Sanhedrin 22a), I lost all pleasure. I accept Hashem's decree. I cannot answer any Sh'eilos now, the tears make me unable to read.... I am unable to eat or keep down any food.... I cannot daven without distraction or even learn a simple topic."... I did all that was in my power to care for my wife and keep her alive, and now I am weak and

in grave danger. I was unable to eat or keep down any food, I could not sleep. Thank God some of the medications have helped a little. I could not daven without distraction and could not learn a simple topic of Gemarah.... Even if I were to accept to marry your proposed suggestion, it would not be worth anything as I am not considered mentally stable enough to agree .... please give me time to regain my composure and clear thinking..."

Six months later, he accepted the match with his 16-year-old niece, to whom he was wed for 39 years, in a marriage that produced 13 children who survived into adulthood. When she too passed away, he was again broken, and passed away little more than a year later at age 75 in Posen (September 23, 1837).

Rav Akiva Eiger, the *Godol HaDor*, could not even learn a page of Gemarah because the crushing pain of his loss of his loved one was so intense.

Why Parshas Acharei Mos on Yom Kippur, and not Parshas Shemini?

The *Shulchan Aruch*: Section 621 *Hilchos Yom KaKippurim, Seder Krias HaTorah*; concerning the order of the Torah Reading for Yom Kippur rules: [After the Morning Service,] two Sifrei Torah scrolls are taken out of the Aron Kodesh. From the first Torah scroll, six men read [passages] from [the beginning of the Torah portion of] *Parshas Acharei Mos...*"

The *Mishneh Berurah* explains that it is stated in the Zohar :

> "*Kol Mi SheMitzTaer Al Misas Bnei Aharon* - that whoever grieves over the deaths of the sons of Aharon;

Grieving & Healing

O Morid Dimaos Aleihem - or sheds tears over them;

Mochlin Lo Avonosav - will have his offenses pardoned;

Uvanav Ainam Meisim BeChayav - and his children will not die in his lifetime."

The deaths of the sons of Aharon HaKohein (Nadav & Avihu) are described in the Torah in two places: (1) in Sefer VaYikra - *Parshas Shemini*; & (2) in Sefer VaYikra - *Parshas Acharei Mos*.

In the 1st version in *Parshas Shemini*, the two sons of Aharon are named: Nadav & Avihu. The Torah reports their deaths in real time - as it's happening: they offered an *"Aish Zarah"* an unauthorized foreign fire to the Mishkan and were burned to death immediately. Aharon HaKohein was silent and Moshe Rabbeinu consoled his brother.

In the 2nd version of the same story, in *Parshas Acharei Mos*, the two sons of Aharon are not named (their identities are merely the sons of Aharon), the Torah summarizes their deaths after-the-fact (hence the name of the Parsha *"Acharei Mos* Shnei Bnei Aharon" - After the deaths of the sons of Aharon). Here, there is no report of their sin, no report of the cause of their deaths, nor Aharon and Moshe's reaction.

So this begs the obvious question: if I am to reflect seriously on Yom Kippur, on the deaths of the sons of Aharon to the point of tears, that it cleanses me of my sins and protects my children from tragedy, wouldn't it make more sense to read the 1st version in *Parshas Shemini* - in real time - to relive the tragedy? Why would the Halacha require us to read the 2nd version that is after-the-fact, from *Parshas Acharei Mos*?

Grieving & Healing

It must be, that there is something unique in the 2nd version of *Parshas Acharei Mos*, that is not to be found in the 1st version of *Parshas Shemini* version. Something so powerful, that it can detonate the secret of God's repentance of Yom Kippur, and can immunize our children from death? What is it?

I would like to suggest that the 2nd version of *Parshas Acharei Mos* contains an editorial that is not contained in the 1st version of *Parshas Shemini*:

> "Hashem spoke to Moshe after the deaths of Aharon's two sons - BeKirvasam El Hashem - when they approached before Hashem and they died."

The *Ohr HaChayim* commentary explains that Aharon HaKohein's sons Nadav & Avihu died *"BeKirvasam El Hashem"* because they got too close to Hashem. Their lives expired because of their extreme devotion to Hashem: *"Sheniskarvu BiDeveikus Gamur LaKodosh Baruch Hu"* Their Dveikus and intimacy with God was so intense, that it was *"Neimus, Areivos, Yedidos, Chavivos, Neshikos & Metikus"* words of great affinity, attachment and closeness.

The *Ohr HaChayim* explains that when Nadav & Avihu served Hashem and performed Mitzvos, their souls were so on fire with love for God, that their Neshamos would reach like flames leaping to the sky, bursting out of their bodies, in an attempt to connect with their Heavenly Father. They didn't go all the way and allow their souls to actually leave their bodies, and it took them great restraint to contain their souls within.

HaRav Yisrael Friedman of Ruzhyn (the Rizhiner Rebbe) compared Nadav & Avihu's holiness to Rebbi Akiva - one of

Grieving & Healing

the 10 Martyrs the "*Eser Harugei Malchus* " who was tragically murdered by the Romans when they tortured him for teaching Torah and combed his skin off his body. According to the Gemarah in Berachos (61b), at the time the Romans were tearing off Reb Akiva's skin he was *Mekabel Ol Malchus Shomayim* - he accepted upon himself the yoke of Heaven and was prepared to give up his life to sanctify Hashem - and his students asked him "*Ad Kahn*" Rebbi, isn't this too much to handle?" Reb Akiva answered: "all my life I was troubled by my inability to fulfil the Mitzvah of being prepared to give one's life for Hashem. Until now. He then recited Krias Shema while being tortured and his soul departed from his body when he got to the word Echad. The Rizhiner Rebbe explained that Reb Akiva was able to be *MeDabek* and cling his soul "*BeDeveikus Niflaah*" to the point of almost death (just like Nadav & Avihu). But because of the Mitzvah of *VeChai Bahem* - that one must live, Reb Akiva performed his Mitzvos with such a holy fire and intensity from within, that his soul would leap out of his body to cling to Hashem (but not all the way) *Ad Klus Hanefesh*. A hairbreadth short of death.

But now that the evil Romans were actually killing him, and there was not going to be a tomorrow, Reb Akiva no longer had the Mitzvah of *VeChai Bahem* and therefore Reb Akiva was able to say *Krias Shema* with total perfection (unlike in the past where he held back) and he was able to "go all the way" with total and complete and unimpeded devotion and Deveikus to Hashem until his soul actually departed from his body.

Yes, the Romans killed Reb Akivah - but he controlled the

narrative and he relinquished his soul on his terms, saying the word Echad completing the Shema - in an ultimate act of *"BeDeveikus Niflaah."*

Thus bringing beautiful meaning to our daily prayer: "VeHoEr Einenu BeSorasecha; *VeDabek* Libeinu BeMitzvosecha." We ask Hashem to connect our hearts to his Mitzvos.

According to HaRav Gedalyah Schorr, this too, explains the deaths of Nadav & Avihu. As it says in the 2nd version of *Parshas Acharei Mos*, they died *"BeKirvasam El Hashem"* because of their extreme and intense Deveikus to Hashem. Their physical bodies could not contain their powerful souls. They served Hashem with their souls literally (almost) leaving their bodies to cling to God.

This is why the Torah in the *Parshas Acharei Mos* version uses a double-Loshon: Acharei Mos and then *"VaYamusu."* They (almost) died whenever they served Hashem in the past, but by this time, they came so close to Hashem, closer than ever before, this time they remained dead, instead of them returning their souls to their bodies. Now, they relinquished their souls and ultimately died. Hence, Acharei Mos and then *"VaYamusu."*

Says HaRav Gedalyah Schorr, this explains the point in the Torah that Nadav & Avihu sinned *"Asher Lo Tzivuy"* they did something that they were not commanded to do. Whenever they did a Mitzvah that they were commanded to do in the Torah, their souls temporarily left to cling to Hashem; but the merit of the Mitzvah that Hashem commanded them to do, served as a spiritual safeguard that caused them to fall short of actually dying, and cause their souls to return to their bodies. The Mitzvah, having been commanded, was their lifeline that brought them back to life. But here, since they were not commanded to bring the foreign fire sacrifice, they were *Ainu Mitzuveh* - they did not have the protections of a Mitzvah, they didn't have the protections of *VeChai Bahem*, and therefore without the protection of the Mitzvah, nor the protections of *VeChai Bahem*, so that their souls were free to leave their bodies out of pure Deveikus, with no safeguards, that they were able to relinquish their souls.

"V"

This concept of being close to Hashem, having Deveikus to God, is of profound significance to me on Hindy's Yahrtzeit.

On March 15, 1998, Hindy celebrated her becoming a *Bas Mitzvah*. She gave a wonderful speech about what the letters of the words: "*Bas Mitzva*" meant to her, that it represented some of the *Midos* that would one day define her personality once she would become an adult [Her speech is reprinted in full at the end of this article].

She broke down the letters of the word *B-A-S*:

> B stood for *Beauty*;
>
> A stood for *Ambition*;
>
> S stood for *Sensitivity*.

She further broke down the letters of the word *M-I-T-Z-V-A*:

> M stood for *Meaning*;

I stood for *Independence*;

T stood for *Truth*;

Z stood for *Zealousness*;

... and when she got to the letter "V" Hindy wrote:

"*V = Velcro:* "I want to be attached to *Hashem's Torah & Mitzvos* like pieces of velcro to one another. I want to stick to *Hashem* and be the best that I can be, and let no one pull me away from *Torah & Mitzvos*."

A = Achievement

I believe that Hindy was "connected" in so many ways, and as a 12-year old girl, she already possessed the emotional maturity and intelligence and wisdom of an adult, to yearn to cling to God, even in the most trying of times.

Are you Looking in, or Looking Out?

Going back to the question, if I am to reflect seriously on the deaths of the sons of Aharon to the point of tears, wouldn't it make more sense to read the version in *Parshas Shemini* - in real time? Why does the Halacha require us to read the version that is after-the-fact, from *Parshas Acharei Mos*? *Morai VeRabbosai*, I would like to suggest the following:

I believe that the Halacha is sending us an incredibly powerful message: and that is, that hard times hit us all. No one is spared from tough times or pain. No one. But the real barometer of gaging how we're doing after a setback, how we're surviving, how we're coping, how we're transcending the test, is what is contained in *Parshas Acharei Mos* and that is "*BeKirvasam El*

Grieving & Healing

Hashem." How close are we to Hashem?

When we stand at Neilah before the end of Yom Kippur during the last final moments, watching as the Gates of Repentance close, do we perceive ourselves as standing outside of the city gates, looking in as the gates close, leaving us, on the outside? Or do we view ourselves standing within the city gates, from within, feeling God's heavenly embrace and love as the gates close as a divine hug keeping us in his Kingdom for just another minute, for just another second of closeness to Him? Where are we? How close are we?

Our focus is not on our tragedies, and not on the past. We don't dwell on our pain. We read the Torah portion on Yom Kippur from *Parshas Acharei Mos* about our intimacy with God now. It's about *"BeKirvasam El Hashem."* How close are we to Hashem - now?

That's the genius behind the Halacha. That's why we read *Parshas Acharei Mos* on Yom Kippur.

A Carrot, an Egg, and a Cup of Coffee

A young woman went to her mother and told her about her life and how things were so hard for her. She did not know how she was going to make it and wanted to give up. She was tired of fighting and struggling. It seemed, that as one problem was solved, a new one arose.

Her mother took her to the kitchen. She filled three pots with water and placed each on a high fire. Soon the pots came to boil. In the first pot she placed carrots, in the second pot she placed eggs, and in the last pot she placed ground coffee beans.

Grieving & Healing

She let them sit and boil, without saying a word.

Turning to her daughter, she asked, "Tell me, what do you see?" "Carrots, eggs, and coffee," she replied.

In about twenty minutes she turned off the burners. She fished the carrots out and placed them in a bowl. She pulled the eggs out and placed them in a bowl. Then she ladled the coffee out and placed it in a bowl.

Turning to her daughter, she asked, "Tell me, what do you see?" "Carrots, eggs, and coffee," she replied.

Her mother brought her closer and asked her to feel the carrots. She did and noted that they were soft. The mother then asked the daughter to take an egg and break it. After pulling off the shell, she observed the hard boiled egg. Finally, the mother asked the daughter to sip the coffee. The daughter smiled as she tasted its rich aroma. The daughter then asked, "What does it mean, mother?"

Her mother explained that each of these objects had faced the exact same adversity and trauma ... boiling water. But each reacted differently. The carrot went in strong, hard, and unrelenting. However, after being subjected to the boiling water, it softened and became weak. The egg had been fragile. Its thin outer shell had protected its liquid interior, but after sitting through the boiling water, its inside became hardened. The ground coffee beans were unique, however. After they were in the boiling water, they had changed the water.

"Which are you?" she asked her daughter. "When adversity knocks on your door, how do you respond? Are you a carrot, an egg or a coffee bean?"

Grieving & Healing

Think of this: Which am I? Am I the carrot that seems strong, but with pain and adversity do I wilt and become soft and lose my strength? Am I the egg that starts with a malleable heart, but changes with the heat? Did I have a fluid spirit, but after a death, a breakup, a financial hardship or some other trial, or pain, have I become hardened and stiff and unapproachable? Does my shell look the same, but on the inside am I bitter and tough with a stiff spirit and hardened heart?

Or am I like the coffee bean? The bean actually changes the hot water, the very circumstance that brings the pain. When the water gets hot, it releases the fragrance and flavor. If you are like the bean, when things are at their worst, you get better and change the situation around you. When the hour is the darkest and trials are their greatest, do you elevate yourself to another level? How do you handle adversity? Are you a carrot, an egg or a coffee bean?

May you have enough happiness to make you sweet, enough trials to make you strong, enough sorrow to keep you human and enough hope to make you happy.

Bilah HaMoves Lanetzach, Umacha Hashem Elokim Dimah Meyal Kol Ponim - May He swallow up death forever; may Hashem wipe away tears from every face (Isaiah 25:8) *T'hei Nishmasa Tzrurah B'tzror Ha'chaim.*

March 10, 1998: Hindy's Speech on the Meaning of Bas Mitzvah

"On March 15, 1998, I will celebrate my becoming a *Bas Mitzva* with my family and friends. The letters of the words:

Grieving & Healing

"*Bas Mitzva*" represent some of the *Midos* that will hopefully define my personality once I become an adult. I have chosen to work hard at improving the following:

B = Beauty: I believe that beauty goes beneath the skin. To me, a truly beautiful person isn't defined by her physical appearance, but is to be appreciated by her sterling character. For example, when the *Torah* introduced us to our mother, Rachel *Imeinu*, the *Posuk* said that she was: "*Yefas Toar Viphas Mareh*" - fair in appearance. The great *Yalkut Shemoni* explains that she was beautiful because she was *Gomel Chesed* to her sister Leah, when she gave her the signals under the *Chupa* to avoid embarrassment. Like Rachel, I want to be known as having beautiful *Midos*.

A = Ambition: I have strong desire to achieve something important with my life. For example I have set a very high standard of scholarship for myself, in that I hope to complete the hole *Tanach (Torah, Neviim & Kesuvim)* by the time I'm 20. I am determined to do what *Hashem* tells me, even if it gets difficult and makes no sense. I believe that *Hashem* will show me the right way and make it easier to follow Him. Just like in *Parshas Teruma*, we see that *Moshe Rabbeinu* tried and tried and tried to build the *Menorah* until *Hashem* finally showed him how to make it. Up until this point in my life, it's been pretty easy to follow in *Hashem's* ways. *Mitzvos* were spoon-fed to me, my whole life, and all of my *Aveiros* went to my parents. Now that I am *Bas Mitzva*, and I am responsible for my actions, I am going to make sure that my personal record is complete with *Mitzvos* and accomplishments.

S = Sensitivity: Sensitivity is very important to

Grieving & Healing

me. Not only should I be sensitive to my own feelings, but I should be extra sensitive to the feelings of others. Just like our *Imahos* & our *Avos* were.

M = *Meaning:* I want my life to be meaningful, and that means, that I want a life full of *Hashem's Mitzvos*. I don't want my birthdays to simply come and go without there being an important accomplishment in my life to make it special. I want the years, the months, the weeks, the days, the minutes, and even the seconds of my life to be important. Especially now that I am a *Bas Mitzva*, and all my *Mitzvos* count, I cannot afford to throw away a single *Mitzvah*. We can see that from all our *Chachomim* and *Rabanim,* who try to make every moment meaningful, doing everything that comes their way *B'simcha*.

I = *Independence:* In the past, if I messed up, my parents assured me that it was OK to goof, and that there's always a next time. While it's still OK for an adult to mess up every once in a while (after all, they are human too), nevertheless, now that I am turning *Bas Mitzva*, I must take complete responsibility for my actions and make sure I am doing the right thing. I am starting over pure and new, with a clean *Neshama*.

T = *Truth:* Truth is very important to me because my friendships and relationships must be built on *Emes* (truth). I cannot exist with *Sheker* (lies). As the *Torah* says in *Parshas Mishpatim*, "*Midbar Sheker Tirchak*" - distance yourself from a lie. I believe this means that I must be truthful even when it is difficult. Only truth is the path to being a true *Bas Yisroel*.

Z   =   *Zealousness:* It's not just the quantity of *Mitzvos* that is important to me, but it is also the quality of them that interests me. I want my *Yiddishkeit* to be alive with electricity. I do not want to be bored with *Davening*, and learning *Chumash*. I want my *Davening* to be "on fire," and I want my learning to be exciting. I think it is very good to do everything in life *B'Zrizus*. Just like *Moshe Rabbeinu*, whenever *Hashem* told him to do something, he did with zealousness.

V   =   *Velcro:*   I want to be attached to *Hashem's Torah & Mitzvos* like pieces of velcro to one another. I want to stick to *Hashem* and be the best that I can be, and let no one pull me away from *Torah & Mitzvos*.

A   =   *Achievement:* I want to achieve in whatever *Hashem* tells me to do. Whatever I do in life, I want to be the best at it. I want to reach the greatest, most powerful goals. Learning *Torah* & keeping *Mitzvos*."

Grieving & Healing

Comments at the Kiddush of Chaya Chana Hindy, May 1, 2017

Thank you for coming to the Kiddush in honor of my 1st granddaughter. Her parents Yechiel &Tali Hertz named their daughter "Hindy" and her full Hebrew name is "Chaya Chana Hinde" which means Chana Hinde lives.

Baby Hindy is named after my daughter Hindy who's soul was returned to Hashem at age 17.5 after a 2.5 year illness 13 years ago. Having the baby named Hindy is indeed a partial consolation and Nechama.

If I could capture the moment, and compare it to a Torah event it is this:

Yaakov Avinu grieved excessively for (what he thought was) his deceased son Yosef for 22 years. He was inconsolable during this time and his grief and sadness permeated every aspect of his life. The Torah barely cites anything about his nondescript life during this time due to his profound sadness, as the gift of prophecy escaped him due to lack of Simcha. .

But that sadness quickly evaporated as Yaakov's granddaughter Serach bas Asher informed him of the great news and Mazal Tov of Yosef (that he was alive). The Torah records that (Sefer Bereishis, Parshas Vayigash, 45:27); "the spirit of Yaakov was revived" as Simcha joy and happiness returned to him. Indeed, thereafter the next Parsha in the Torah records: "VaYechi Yaakov" that Yaakov (finally) lived life.

This thought resonates within me as this beautiful baby is named Hindy. A cloud lifted; Something inside me opened up allowing the break in the clouds to usher in beacons of light and joy. Mazal tov.

Bais Yaakov of Los Angeles – Hindy Cohen Memorial Fund

On February 23, 2004, our family and the entire Los Angeles community suffered a terrible loss with the untimely passing of our daughter, Hindy ע"ה. Although Hindy was only 17 years old when she died, she had touched and enriched the lives of so many people. Hindy possessed an unswerving belief in *Hashem* and lived each day of her life filled with His *Torah* and *Mitzvos*. Hindy was known for her incredible *Simchas Hachaim* (love of life). It lit up every room that she entered.

Our Hindy was a true Bais Yaakov girl. She was happiest at school with her friends and her teachers whom she loved so much. When thinking about how best to perpetuate Hindy's name, it has always been very clear to us that Hindy would want us to help her school, Bais Yaakov of Los Angeles. Hindy's last *Shabbos* was spent with her friends on the Bais Yaakov Shabbaton in Malibu. When she returned home on *Motzei Shabbos*, Hindy told us how beautiful the *Shabbos* was and how much it meant to her to be there with her friends. The Bais Yaakov Halleli Song & Dance Festival was a program that Hindy also adored. She loved the preparations, the singing, the dancing and the genuine joy of creating something beautiful and meaningful with her friends. Hindy would want us to make sure that these programs along with all the other extras that make Bais Yaakov so special would continue to bring joy to all the girls of BYLA.

It is therefore, with bittersweet tears and a heavy heart that constantly yearns for Hindy's well being that we inaugurated the fund at Bais Yaakov to perpetuate Hindy's memory to various programs of Torah and Chesed here.

Your generous contribution will enable us to keep Hindy's memory alive in all of our hearts, and to elevate her precious *Neshoma* with every act of *Chesed* that is performed on her behalf. Please mail your tax deductible contribution in the enclosed envelope. Checks should be made payable to "Bais Yaakov" and the memorandum on the check should reference the ***Hindy Cohen Memorial Fund.*** In the *Zechus* of all who assist in this noble project, may we be *Zocheh* to share only *Simchos* in the future.

Made in the USA
Columbia, SC
08 January 2018